To Lou, who kept my feet moving forward on life's path,

To Kelly, the love of my life,

To Julianne and Elaine, my reasons for living, and

To my dear friend, Steve, who lives on in the heavens.

# When the Race Was Won

*The Story of NASA's Gemini Program*

ISBN 978-1-7377686-0-9 (hardcover)
ISBN 978-1-7377686-1-6 (paperback)
ISBN 978-1-7377686-2-3 (ebook)

Gray Carlisle Publishing
Floyds Knobs, Indiana

Publisher's Cataloging-in-Publication data

Names: Colomb, Bartley, author.

Title: When the race was won : the story of NASA's Gemini Program / Bart Colomb.
Description: Includes bibliographical references. | Floyds Knobs, IN: Gray Carlisle Publishing, 2021.

Identifiers: LCCN: (PCN): 2021916741 | ISBN: 9781737768609 (hardcover) | 9781737768616 (paperback) | 9781737768623 (ebook)
Subjects: LCSH Project Gemini (U.S.) | United States. National Aeronautics and Space Administration. | Aerospace engineering. | Astronautics. | Space sciences. | Technology. | BISAC SCIENCE / Space Science / Space Exploration | HISTORY / United States / 20th century
Classification: LCC TL789.8.U6 G68 2021 | DDC 629.45/4/0973--dc23

# When the Race Was Won

*The Story of NASA's Gemini Program*

B ART  C OLOMB

**Gray Carlisle** PUBLISHING
Floyds Knobs, Indiana

# Table of Contents

# Acknowledgments

Anyone who has ever started a business from scratch will tell you that such an enterprise is a multi-faceted process that, at certain stages, must literally be willed into being. Creating a concept for a book and then having that idea evolve into a manuscript is a very similar process. That said, this book would still be a jumbled collection of chicken-scratchings on a pile of legal pads in my basement were it not for the hard work and dedication of one person, my dear friend and assistant for nearly three decades, Dina Pease. There is no other living person who, even if they had her incredible skill and patience, could possibly have deciphered the hieroglyphics that are the product of my handwriting and turned them into a viable manuscript. Dina, you are simply the best and I will always be grateful for your loyalty, your dedication, and most of all, your friendship. These last twenty- eight years of my professional life would not have run nearly as smoothly – or been nearly as pleasant – without you.

Thanks also to Adam Robinson at Good Book Developers.com. Your kindness and professionalism in guiding this literary rookie through the stages of turning a raw manuscript into an actual book will not be forgotten.

If I have a regret with regard to the book, it is that in order to keep the story from meandering off the track on the flight control side, I was not able to wander very far away from the flight director's console. As a result, there are scores of people, particularly flight controllers, whose stories I would have loved to tell here but could not without making the book unwieldy. If you are interested in learning more about those guys (and I hope you are), I highly recommend two books. First, Go Flight, The Unsung Heroes of Mission Control 1965-1992, by Rick Houston and Milt Heflin.

Also, From the Trenches of Mission Control to the Craters of the Moon, a collection of writings by members of the remarkable brotherhood of first-row flight controllers in the Mercury Control Center at the Cape and, later, Mission Control in Houston. The latter work contains the personal memoirs of legendary flight director Glynn Lunney whose contributions to the Gemini program are chronicled here.

Also, to the people who are profiled in the following pages who are alive today and to the descendants of those who are not, I have tried to portray you or your loved one in an honest, balanced, and most importantly, historically accurate way. If you believe that I have not done so, please accept my assurance that any injustice which you believe that I have done to you or to him was not a deliberate act on my part. Further, any mistakes or inaccuracies set forth on the pages that follow are mine and mine alone and I accept full responsibility for them.

Finally, thank you, the reader. I hope that these pages will take you places where you have never been before with regard to Project Gemini. I also hope that you will enjoy the journey. All the best.

Bart Colomb
May 17, 2021

# Timeline

| | |
|---|---|
| **October 4, 1957** | Soviet Union launches Sputnik 1, first artificial satellite, into orbit. |
| **January 31, 1958** | United States launches Explorer 1, first U.S. satellite, into orbit. |
| **July 29, 1958** | United States creates National Aeronautics and Space Administration (NASA). |
| **April 12, 1961** | First man in space: Single orbit flight of Yuri Gagarin aboard Vostok 1. |
| **May 5, 1961** | First manned flight of NASA's Project Mercury: Suborbital flight of Alan B. Shepard, Jr. aboard Freedom 7. |

| | |
|---|---|
| **May 25, 1961** | President John F. Kennedy commits United States to national goal of landing a man on the moon and returning him safely to the Earth "before this decade is out." |
| **February 20, 1962** | First U.S. orbital flight: John H. Glenn, Jr. aboard Friendship 7. |
| **July 11, 1962** | NASA selects Lunar Orbit Rendezvous (LOR) as method to fly to the moon (i.e. "The Mode"). |
| **May 15-16, 1963** | Final flight of Mercury program: Faith 7, flown by L. Gordon "Gordo" Cooper. |
| **March 18, 1965** | Cosmonaut Alexei Leonov becomes first human being to walk in space. |
| **March 23, 1965** | Gemini 3: First manned Gemini flight crewed by Virgil I. "Gus" Grissom and John W. Young. |

| | |
|---|---|
| **June 3, 1965** | Gemini IV: Edward H. White II becomes first American to walk in space. |
| **August 21-29, 1965** | Gemini V: Eight day duration flight. |
| **December 4-18, 1965** | Gemini 7/6: First rendezvous in space; Fourteen day duration flight. |
| **March 16, 1966** | Gemini VIII: First docking in space. |
| **June 3-6, 1966** | Gemini IX: Second United States EVA. |
| **July 18-21, 1966** | Gemini X: Third U.S. EVA; Second U.S. docking. |
| **September 12-15, 1966** | Gemini XI: Altitude record (850 miles). |

| | |
|---|---|
| **November 11-15, 1966** | Gemini XII: Last flight of the Gemini program; Longest duration EVA. |
| **January 27, 1967** | Apollo 1 fire kills Gus Grissom, Ed White and Roger Chaffee. |
| **October 11-22, 1968** | Apollo 7: First manned Apollo mission commanded by Walter M. Schirra, Jr. |
| **July 20, 1969** | Apollo 11: Neil Armstrong and Buzz Aldrin land lunar module "Eagle" in the Sea of Tranquility; Both men walk on the lunar surface. |
| **July 24, 1969** | Apollo 11 splashes down fulfilling President John F. Kennedy's goal. |
| **December 7-19, 1972** | Apollo 17: Last lunar landing. |

# Prologue

The world changed forever on October 4, 1957. American families, who only the night before had slept comfortably in the security of their Ozzie and Harriet world, were now confronted by a menace circling above them in the heavens. That menace was called Sputnik. Until that moment, Americans had never had any reason to doubt their technological superiority over the Soviet Union. Though Stalin had brought down his Iron Curtain over Eastern Europe after World War II and his socialist regime had always conducted its affairs—particularly those related to weapons technology and development—under a veil of absolute secrecy, the United States had been the first to split the atom and the first to build both the atomic and hydrogen bombs. Even given the Soviet Union's insatiable appetite and considerable aptitude for espionage as well as the fact that they'd already stolen many American innovations, the thought that Russia could best the United States in crucial fields such as satellite technology and rocket lifting capability was simply incomprehensible to the average American. Until now. The relentless beeping radio signal from Sputnik as it orbited above the continental United States was a constant reminder to Americans that their country had been surpassed. The question that resonated through the Eisenhower administration was "Now what?" While the Sputnik launch certainly had both strategic and tactical military implications, the smart money supported the proposition that the ultimate Soviet goal in all this was to put the first man into space. Further, the worldwide propaganda ramifications from such a Cold War coup were almost too devastating for America's leaders to contemplate. It was therefore clear that the Soviets had to be challenged immediately. It fell to Eisenhower to figure out the best way to make that happen.

# PROJECT MERCURY

IKE'S ANSWER WAS THE National Aeronautics and Space Administration (NASA) which came into being on July 29, 1958. After the initial shock of Sputnik, the United States had responded on January 31, 1958 by launching its own orbital satellite named Explorer 1 atop the U.S. Army's Juno I rocket. With that first faltering step, the race was now on to put the first man into space and accomplishing that objective was NASA's sole stated purpose. The creation of Project Mercury, the testing process and selection of the original seven astronauts, the training of those men and, ultimately, the selection of Alan B. Shepard, Jr. to fly the first Mercury mission would all follow in relatively short order. Due to Werner Von Braun's insistence upon exhaustive (some thought excessive) testing of the Mercury/Redstone launch vehicle, Shepard's flight would not be scheduled until May 2, 1961. After NASA had relented to Von Braun's demands, the Soviets stunned NASA, the United States and the rest of western civilization by launching cosmonaut Yuri Gagarin into space. On April 12, 1961, Gagarin successfully flew a spacecraft called Vostok 1 in a single orbit mission around the planet. Having lost another round to the Soviets, the Americans had no choice but to set about the task of catching and, hopefully, one day surpassing their Cold War rival. The space race, as it had come to be called, had begun in earnest.

With the possible exception of John Glenn, it had come as no great surprise to anyone at NASA when program director Bob Gilruth informed the seven astronauts that Al Shepard had been selected to fly the first manned Mercury mission. Because NASA's more powerful Atlas booster had not yet been man-rated, the initial American flight would be a parabolic or "suborbital" mission launched atop the smaller Redstone. Shepard would be catapulted approximately 300 miles downrange and achieve an altitude of 115 miles after which he would reenter Earth's atmosphere and execute a parachute landing in the Atlantic Ocean. The mission, named Freedom 7, flew on May 5, 1961 and was executed flawlessly. It did not match Gargarin's orbital flight but Shepard's fifteen minutes aloft had put the United States in the game. For his efforts, "Big Al" as he came to be known at the Cape, would never again experience anonymity in his lifetime. Not that he minded that very much. Also of importance to his future was the fact that Shepard had firmly entrenched himself at the top of the NASA flight rotation pyramid. It was a position that the ultra-competitive Navy commander had no intention of ever relinquishing.

Due to ongoing development problems with the Atlas (i.e. it kept blowing up during testing at an alarmingly unacceptable rate), it was determined that Mercury's next flight, to be flown by Virgil I. "Gus" Grissom, would be another suborbital mission on the Redstone. Although little was to be gained in the way of data by simply retracing Shepard's flight path, at least NASA could prove to the country and to the Russians that Shepard's flight was not a stunt and that its success was no fluke. Gus flew his spacecraft Liberty Bell 7 beautifully through the suborbital parabola down to a pinpoint landing in the Atlantic. Then things went south. As Gus himself put it, "I was layin' there mindin' my own business when POW, the hatch went and water started pourin' in over the sill." For reasons still being debated, Liberty Bell's hatch had blown off and away from the spacecraft before the rescue helicopter tasked with retrieving it could hook a cable onto it and pull it out of the water. Confronted with the very real possibility of drowning inside the capsule, Grissom bailed out through the open hatch into the ocean. Meanwhile, the ship had taken on so much water that it could not be lifted by the helicopter assigned to retrieve it. Once the pilot blew the cable attached to the Liberty Bell, another helicopter swooped in and dropped a rescue collar to Grissom which he managed to get on before his water-logged spacesuit could finally pull him under. Gus had been saved but Liberty Bell 7 sank to the bottom of the Atlantic. Losing the ship did little to bolster Grissom's previously stellar reputation within NASA. In a competition as fierce as this space race, a mistake of this magnitude—if it was a mistake and not simply a malfunction—was not something the NASA brass was likely to tolerate. Gus now had to hold his breath through an investigation and keep holding it until the rest of the Mercury program played itself out to see where he stood in the future flight rotation—if he had any standing at all.

After the Atlas was finally approved for human spaceflight, NASA's original All-American boy, John H. Glenn, Jr., was chosen to fly the program's first orbital flight. Friendship 7, as Glenn dubbed it, went up on February 20, 1962. By the time it came back down, both man and mission had become the stuff of legend. Part of the myth was that Glenn's flight had to be aborted because Friendship 7's heat shield had somehow been compromised and that Glenn had cheated death all the way down to the North Atlantic. In actuality, a false indicator light in Mercury Control had signaled that the heat shield was loose when it was actually still intact. This had prompted NASA's leadership to insist—over the explicit objection of Flight Director Chris Kraft—that Friendship 7's retrorocket package be left on during reentry ostensibly to hold the spacecraft's heat shield in place. When post-flight inspection of the heat shield revealed that Kraft had been right, Kraft used the meddling of the NASA brass to force them to institute a rule that for all future missions only one man—the Flight Director— would have the authority to make mission critical decisions in real time and that those decisions could not be overruled—not even by the President of the United States. As for Glenn, the fame and adulation afforded him were practically unprecedented in the country's history. Unfortunately, his halo came with a price tag. It was widely rumored that President John F. Kennedy informed NASA that Glenn's life was now far too valuable to be risked on any future space mission. If he went back up and was killed, the devastation to the country might necessitate ending the entire space program. In the process of becoming a national hero, John Glenn had also effectively grounded himself.

Following Glenn's act would not be an easy task for the next guy in line. Initially slotted for the position was the ruggedly–handsome Donald K. Slayton who all at NASA had come to know as "Deke." Only Deke had a serious problem. NASA's medical staff had known for years that Slayton had a cardiac condition which had been diagnosed as paroxysmal atrial fibrillation which, in Deke's case, meant that every so often without reason or warning his heart would skip a beat. Although Slayton had endured the rigorous selection and training process that all of the Mercury astronauts had gone through and had shown himself to be more than fit for those tasks, NASA's higher-ups were now getting cold feet when confronted with the reality of actually having to send Deke into space. If Slayton should suffer some sort of cardiac event in flight and he died before NASA could get him back down, it would undoubtedly result in a worldwide public relations cataclysm from which NASA might not ever recover. So, in typical ass-covering bureaucratic fashion, NASA grounded Deke and handed the flight over to Malcolm S. "Scott" Carpenter. After it had all played out (and Carpenter had nearly become the original inspiration for Tom Hanks' character in Cast Away), the NASA brass probably wished that they'd sent Deke up and risked the heart attack.

Aurora 7, which Carpenter's mission was named, was beset by difficulties from the outset. Many, if not most, of the problems were caused by Carpenter himself. Driven by his scientific curiosity to look at various sights which were not scheduled for observation in the Aurora 7 flight plan, Carpenter began to use Aurora's small thrusters in a cavalier fashion to position the craft so that he could see all of the things that he wanted to see. This in turn led to excessive fuel consumption. All the while, Carpenter's continual inflight maneuvering had made Chris Kraft absolutely livid back in Mercury Control. Matters got worse when it became apparent that Scott did not have enough fuel left to make a controlled reentry and that he was going to have to bring the ship down through the Earth's atmosphere manually. Carpenter made it through but Kraft would later recall, "It was uncanny luck that he survived. He was goddamned lucky it didn't come down bass–ackwards because it could have. Somebody was looking out for him." Still, though he'd somehow managed to survive until splashdown, Scott had also overshot the landing zone and primary recovery forces by some 250 nautical miles. When the choppers finally located him,

Scott was sitting calmly in a life raft beside the Aurora. Perhaps he was contemplating the wonders he'd just experienced. Back in Mercury Control, Chris Kraft had no need for any sort of contemplation because he'd already made up his mind. As long as Kraft had breath in his body, there was no way that Scott Carpenter would ever fly for NASA again.

To add insult to injury, less than three months after NASA had labored to get Carpenter through three orbits, the Soviets sent up Andriyan Nikolayev in Vostok 3 on August 11, 1962. It was the first Russian flight since Gherman Titov had orbited the Earth 17 times the previous year. Then, for good measure, they sent Pavel Popovich up in Vostok 4 the next damned *day*. Even worse, Popovich had come within four miles of Nicolayev while in orbit and the two had simultaneously conversed with one another and the ground during the flight. That smelled a lot like orbital rendezvous and, if it was, it meant that the Soviet program was likely years ahead of NASA. Of course, Soviet Premier Nikita Khrushchev was happy to let the West assume the worst—and it did. It was not known until years later that the proximity in orbit achieved by the two Russian spacecraft was due to the precision of their launches and not because either of the Vostoks had the capability to maneuver in space. Still, by the time the Russians finally brought the two cosmonauts down, Nicolayev had orbited the Earth a jaw-dropping 64 times.

After Mr. Carpenter's wild ride had followed Liberty Bell 7's voyage to the bottom of the sea, NASA would require a much steadier hand in the cockpit during the next flight if the brass didn't want Kennedy or members of Congress to start asking questions that they didn't like having to answer. Enter Walter M. "Wally" Schirra. Wally, admittedly disappointed by not being assigned to an earlier mission, had kept his head down and worked diligently while waiting for his name to be called. That happened on October 3, 1962 when he went up in Sigma 7. Flying a textbook mission, Wally achieved the ultimate six orbit goal of the program which neither Glenn or Carpenter had been able to attain. Capping it all off with a beautiful precision landing during which he nearly hit the bridge of the recovery carrier, Wally had positioned himself well for even bigger and better things in NASA's future.

With Schirra's unqualified success on Sigma 7, it appeared to be an opportune time for NASA to pull the plug on Project Mercury. The only problem was that they still had a capsule left and an astronaut, L. Gordon "Gordo" Cooper, who hadn't yet flown a mission. Although Gordo was undeniably a terrific pilot, there were reasons why he was the last of the original seven to be chosen to fly. As Slayton would say in later years, Gordo "didn't show the best judgment at times." Proving Deke's point, after it was announced that Cooper's flight in space would last a full day, far beyond the Mercury spacecraft's original design limits, Gordo irritated the daylights out of the NASA brass by announcing that he was naming the spacecraft "Faith 7." Then, to make sure they stayed mad, he took an F-102 in low during an unscheduled flight a day before the launch at the Cape and came so close to the administration office that he nearly blew the windows out of the building. That, in turn, caused Mercury Chief of Operations Walt Williams, who was inside the building at the time, to nearly hit the roof. As Shepard later recounted, "When Walt looked out the window (which was on the building's second floor), here was this jet streaking by *below* his altitude." After a trip to the men's room to clean out his trousers, Williams was on the phone to Shepard screaming that Gordo was finished at NASA and that he was pulling him off the flight of Faith 7. Fortunately for Gordo, after Slayton had been grounded, the remaining Mercury astronauts had come up with a plan for Deke's future at NASA.

One of the things that NASA had absolutely not anticipated was the stratospheric level of fame that the Mercury astronauts would attain. Along with that notoriety would come an intense level of curiosity about and scrutiny of their private lives. NASA desperately wanted to portray the group to the press and the public as the All-American white knights of the space age. The problem was that none of them except Glenn could even remotely come close to living up to that image. In truth, this was a hard-drinking Corvette-racing bunch of test pilots which included at least a couple of guys to whom marital fidelity was something of an abstract concept. Although fully aware of that, NASA still demanded that the guys toe the agency's puritanical line. Also knowing that at least some of them were likely to rebel against that demand, NASA hit upon the idea of having an Army general chaperone their activities like some sort of den mother. Since, as Deke said, that went over "like a turd in a punch bowl," that's when the idea of possibly tapping Slayton to supervise the astronauts began to take shape. Schirra summarized the group's attitude when he recalled, "Do we want an outsider to do this or do we want Deke to do it?" In a move that Slayton later described as the other six throwing him a bone and solving the chaperone problem all in one neat package, Deke won hands down over the general and became chief of the newly formed Astronaut Office. The decision to put Deke there was one that would have a profound impact on NASA flight crew operations over the next decade. However, the most immediate consequence of the decision was that dealing with Cooper was no longer Walt Williams' job, it was now Slayton's and he knew damn well that pulling Gordo off the flight would kill his NASA career. So Deke stood firm against Williams and the other NASA honchos after Gordo's scalp and kept him in the cockpit for Faith 7. Cooper rewarded Deke's loyalty by steadily flying Faith 7 for 22 orbits before splashing down on May 16, 1963. Gordo would be the last American to go into orbit alone.

Unfortunately, if anyone at NASA felt like popping champagne corks after Cooper's flight, it didn't take the Russians long to spoil the party. Less than a month after Gordo splashed down, they sent up Valery Bykovsky in Vostok 5 on June 14, 1963. Bykovsky would stay up five days and orbit the Earth an incredible 82 times. But Khrushchev's real coup-de-grace came two days after Bykovsky's launch when the Soviets sent up Valentina Tereshkova in Vostok 6 making her the first human female to fly in space. At the end of her 48 orbit mission on June 19th, Khrushchev exercised absolutely no restraint in pointing out to the world that the flight time of all the American astronauts in Project Mercury combined had been surpassed by a single Russian *WOMAN.*

# THE MODE

BEFORE PROJECT MERCURY HAD ever launched a spacecraft, debate had been stirring in NASA's highest echelons over the most viable method to put an American on the moon and return him safely to Earth. Now, in order to fulfill the national goal President Kennedy had outlined during a speech to a Joint Session of Congress just days after Al Shepard's flight, they were confronted with the additional burden of having to do it by the end of the decade. This method, whatever it would eventually come to be, was known within NASA as "The Mode."

Since the days of Oberth, Tsiolkovsky and Goddard, the way that the visionaries had imagined going to the moon involved placing a man on top of a huge rocket and blasting him straight to it. Once there, he would land and then blast back off the lunar surface and return to Earth in the same vehicle in which he began the journey. This somewhat spartan theory came to be known as "Direct Ascent." As time passed and the complexity of lifting matter off of the Earth's surface into space became better understood, it had become increasingly obvious that Direct Ascent just wasn't going to work because any single spacecraft carrying enough fuel to generate the thrust necessary to first blast out of the Earth's atmosphere and back up off the lunar surface after the landing was going to be much too large to safely land on the moon. As NASA engineer John Houbolt said in later years, "Down at the Cape, they needed three or four thousand people to launch an Atlas. These people were talking about landing something the size of an Atlas on the surface of the moon backward with no help whatsoever. I thought that was preposterous." Indeed it was. While the internal debate raged at NASA, Houbolt happened upon a report which had come out of Langley proposing that the landing be conducted using a method that the Langley guys called "Lunar Orbit Rendezvous" or LOR.

The guiding principle of LOR was that two separate smaller spacecraft would be required for the lunar voyage. Further, that they would be launched into space atop a large multi-stage rocket of which each section would fall away once the fuel in that stage had been consumed. Then the two vehicles would fly out to the moon while docked together. Once in lunar orbit, the ships would separate and one would fly down to the moon's surface and land. In order for the plan to work, it became obvious early on that the vehicle tasked with landing on the moon had to be as lightweight as possible and thus had to be stripped down to three basic essentials: (1) enough fuel for the descent from lunar orbit down to the lunar surface; (2) a navigable vehicle with a habitable living space for two astronauts to survive for up to three days with enough space to stow their equipment and consumables for the stay on the surface; and (3) enough fuel to get back up off the surface and into lunar orbit. The vehicle to be used solely for the lunar landing would come to be designated as the Lunar Excursion Module or "LM." The beauty of conducting the landing in the LM (and of LOR) was that it would not be necessary to take the weight of the entire expedition's provisioning down to the lunar surface and blast it back up for the return voyage to Earth. All of that equipment and rationing would remain parked in lunar orbit in the second ship which was to be designated as the Command and Service Module or "CSM."

Although LOR was initially regarded by many at NASA as a far-out scheme, Houbolt was unfazed and almost immediately became LOR's most ardent supporter. As factions emerged, it became increasingly clear that in addition to disliking Houbolt's proposal, many in NASA's upper echelons (foremost among them chief spacecraft designer Maxime Faget) simply didn't like Houbolt himself. Regardless, with the drawbacks of Direct Ascent coming more sharply into focus, the NASA masterminds had to rethink the problem and give appropriate consideration to Houbolt's approach—whether they liked Houbolt or not. Eventually, on July 11, 1962, Houbolt won out and NASA announced that Lunar Orbit Rendezvous had been chosen as "The Mode" for their attempt to land an American on the moon by the beginning of the 1970s.

Had Direct Ascent been found to be viable, "all" NASA would have needed to do to fly to the moon was: (a) build a rocket powerful enough to blast a spacecraft out of Earth orbit with enough additional fuel to propel it to the moon and back; (b) build a spacecraft that could withstand the rigors of the voyage to the moon and back; (c) prove that a human being could survive in space for the approximate fourteen day time period it was thought would be required to make the journey; and (d) build a suit that would allow an astronaut to leave the vehicle and perform whatever tasks NASA deemed necessary on the lunar surface. With LOR now the chosen mode, more layers would have to be added to the overall planning of the mission.

Using the LOR two vehicle mode, once at the moon in lunar orbit, the mission commander would separate the LM from the CSM, fly it down to the lunar surface and land. Next, after all planned activity on the surface was completed, the ascent stage of the LM would blast off the lunar surface and attain lunar orbit. Then, the LM astronauts had to be able to find or "rendezvous" with the CSM. Then the two vehicles would have to physically join safely together or "dock" so that the LM crew could safely transfer back inside the CSM. The ascent stage of the LM would then be jettisoned and the crew would blast out of lunar orbit and return to Earth in the CSM, which alone would be equipped with a heat shield.

It was these additional engineering requirements over and above those of Direct Ascent that necessitated the creation and implementation of Project Gemini. Direct Ascent would have required both long duration flight and extravehicular activity (EVA). With LOR now the chosen mode, NASA had to address the additional requirements of rendezvous and docking. Moreover, they were certainly going to need to test their proposed solutions to those problems extensively in Earth orbit before ever daring to try them around the moon. It was in this way that the operational goals of NASA's "Bridge to the Moon" had come to be defined. To cross it, Project Gemini would have to prove definitively that long duration flight of up to fourteen days, rendezvous between two vehicles in space, docking of those vehicles in space and EVA were all possible. If NASA failed to accomplish any of them, there was a very real possibility that the first flag planted on the lunar surface would prominently feature a hammer and a sickle.

# ON TO GEMINI

WITH SO MANY GEMINI objectives, it looked as if the program was going to require at least ten manned missions. Facing the increasing likelihood that at least a couple of the original seven astronauts were not going to fly after Project Mercury, it was becoming readily apparent that those who remained were simply not going to be able to adequately man the necessary flight rotation required to fulfill the program's objectives. In short, NASA needed more astronauts. NASA introduced the Group 2 astronauts on September 17, 1962. During their individual careers the "New Nine" would run the gamut from being figures of global historical significance to American heroes to tragic figures whose names relatively few knew in the 1960s and even fewer can recall today. Their names, in alphabetical order, were: Neil Armstrong, Frank Borman, Charles "Pete" Conrad, James Lovell, James McDivitt, Elliot See, Thomas P. Stafford, Edward White and John W. Young.

Now that the program objectives were defined and NASA had enough astronauts to move forward, it became necessary to choose a spacecraft and a launch vehicle. As the Mercury capsules had all performed in an exemplary fashion (Liberty Bell 7's hatch notwithstanding), the choice to leave McDonnell Aircraft in St. Louis in charge of spacecraft production was a relatively simple one. For Gemini, McDonnell enlarged the cockpit to accommodate two astronauts and added an equipment module known as the "adapter section" to contain critical systems below the base of the heat shield which would, of course, be jettisoned prior to reentry. Because the escape tower system employed by Mercury was to be replaced by ejection seats on Gemini, the Atlas had to be eliminated as a launch vehicle because its liquid oxygen/kerosene fuel mix was so combustible (think "napalm") that an ejection seat could not clear it in the event of an explosion or breakup during a failed launch attempt. Chosen to replace the Atlas was the two stage heavy intercontinental ballistic missile Titan II which had been developed by the Martin Company. The first stage of the Titan II was fueled by a far less volatile mix of hydrazine-based

Aerozin 50 and nitrogen tetroxide which was hypergolic meaning that the two substances would ignite on contact with one another and required no independent ignition source.

Once the issues of mode, spacecraft and launch vehicle had been squared away, the question then remaining was: Who was going to command the initial mission? With Slayton now firmly entrenched as the Chief of Flight Crew Operations, everyone at the Cape already knew the answer to that question. As Slayton would later recall, "It was Al Shepard all the way. I wouldn't have had it any other way. God knows neither would Al."

Alan Bartlett Shepard, Jr. was born on November 18, 1923. His father, called Bart, served with the AEF in World War I and joined the Army Reserves in 1918. Eventually, he would attain the rank of colonel which is how young Alan and his sister Polly addressed him. Their mother Renza was the fun parent. As a young child, Alan had a knack for making friends and then discarding them for no apparent reason. Also mischievous, one Christmas he presented a cigar to Bart's older brother which after being lit promptly exploded in Uncle Fritz's face. Needless to say, The Colonel was not amused. Eventually, Alan's frenetic energy was harnessed into a fascination with airplanes fueled in no small measure by his bearing witness to the celebrity and national adulation showered upon Charles Lindbergh in the decade after his historic transatlantic flight. Also, by the mid-1930s the Navy was starting to land planes on ships—"aircraft carriers" they called them—and Alan took notice of that as well.

Deciding not to follow in his father's footsteps, Alan opted instead for the U.S. Naval Academy in Annapolis where he enrolled on June 19, 1941. After earning his commission, Shepard was selected in 1950 to join the elite Navy Test Pilot School at Patuxent River Air Station. Following two tours at "Pax River", Al had established himself as one of the Navy's finest test pilots. He would parlay that experience into an invitation to try out for NASA's newly formed astronaut corps and was informed that he'd been accepted for Project Mercury on April 1, 1959. From there, Freedom 7 had followed and command of the first Gemini mission awaited.

While that was all unfolding, Al's robust personality and zest for living would enable him to blend seamlessly into the Cape Canaveral landscape of NASA's early years. It was a culture of one-upmanship that featured almost daily battles to determine who could drive the fastest or drink the most. Included in that environment was the exchange of a plethora of practical jokes. Pursuant to the rules of the game, the more elaborate the prank and the more unsuspecting the victim, the greater the esteem accorded the perpetrator. While inhabiting that insular world, Al would leave an indelible mark on everyone who crossed his path. One of those people was a guy in the pocket-protector brigade who wanted play in the big leagues and convinced himself it would be a hoot to pop the lock on Al's Corvette and then fill it from floorboard to ceiling with scores of the big boxy Kotex pads of the era. The guy then retreated to the safety of his office where he and the rest of the geek squad roared their approval while watching Al pluck them all out. The moron was still basking in his triumph over "Big Al" a couple of weeks later when he got a call out of the blue from launch complex leader Guenter Wendt, an intense German transplant who when on his game could scare the living shit out of pretty much anyone at NASA. Guenter then proceeded to inform him that there was a problem with one of his systems down at the launchpad. When the guy asked what kind of problem, Wendt screamed in his Prussian field marshal accent, "The kind that if it's not corrected immediately, you'll find a pink slip in your mailbox at the end of the day!" before slamming down the phone. The guy dropped the receiver and ran straight to his car and began cranking the engine only to find that it wouldn't start. Now frantic, he sprinted back into the building where he found Al with his sport jacket slung over a shoulder standing in the lobby. As the guy breathlessly explained his dilemma, Al said quite sympathetically, "Calm down, pal. Here's my keys. Take the 'Vette down to the pad and bring it back once you've got everything lined out." After thanking Al profusely, the guy sprinted out to Al's Corvette, hopped in and took off. Al then let him clear the main gate before he picked up the phone and called the Cocoa Beach Police to report that the vehicle had just been stolen. As even Barney Fife could've collared "the guy flying down the causeway in Al Shepard's Corvette," the police had their man in custody within minutes. After the poor guy told his side of the story, a police dispatcher called Al, told him the guy's name and asked Al if he'd loaned him the car. Al said, "Let me think a second ... nope, that name doesn't ring a bell" and hung up. Al then proceeded to let the guy roast in the Cocoa Beach jail for six *hours* (with the guy still not knowing that the call from Wendt was a fake or that Al had removed the battery from his car) before calling the dispatcher back and saying that the whole thing had been a misunderstanding. Everyone at the Cape got the message—you didn't mess around with Big Al Shepard. Well, everyone except the proprietor of a Cocoa Beach motel who, during a heated argument with Shepard, took it upon himself to call Al a "motherfucker." When the guy went out to skim the fenced-in and padlocked motel pool the next morning he unlocked the gate and walked inside only to find himself having a shinbone-to-eyeball Come-to-Jesus with a six foot Florida alligator which had somehow managed to get inside the fenced-in padlocked pool area. Yeah, you just didn't ...well, you get the picture.

With his reputation as the King of the Cape cemented by those incidents and many others like them, Al now only needed to await NASA's official announcement of his command of the first Gemini mission to formalize his coronation. Or so he thought. Then, the unimaginable happened to Alan Shepard. As he described it, "I got up to go to the bathroom one morning and completely lost my balance...I thought to myself, 'Gee I didn't really have that much to drink last night.'" Unfortunately for Al, it wasn't a hangover. It was instead the vertiginous manifestation of Meniere's disease, a disorder of the inner ear which the medical experts of the time had deemed to be incurable. After a course of diuretics and other medications failed to bring Al's symptoms under control, NASA grounded him.

Seeing his pal in distress, Slayton soon persuaded Shepard to take a position helping Deke run the Astronaut Office. Deke's decision to bring Al on board was one that would come to impact many (if not all) who would follow the Mercury Seven into the astronaut corps. Al had never been the most congenial guy, at least to people of his own gender, to begin with and the Meniere's ordeal had only served to make him even more volatile. As many astronauts would come to learn the hard way in the years ahead, the last guy you wanted to run into in a NASA hallway was a grounded Al Shepard.

With Deke and Al now running the show in the Astronaut Office, it was time for the United States to fire the next volley in the race to the moon. Unfortunately, before they could get it off, the Soviets let go with one of their own. Khrushchev had always been perhaps the greatest beneficiary of the openness with which the American space program was conducted and he was completely aware that the next phase of the United States program called for sending up a two-man spacecraft called Gemini. For their part, Soviet engineers and mission planners had also intended to send up a two-man vehicle called Voskhod. However, in light of NASA's stated Gemini plan, Voskhod as it was currently envisioned was not going to be a big enough leap forward to satiate the bombastic Soviet premier. So he ordered that Voskhod 1 be completely stripped down to make the spacecraft habitable for *three* men so that when Gemini went up the Soviets could declare that they had already bested the Americans by flying three men to their two.

While the utter childishness of Khrushchev's antics was bad enough, his demands also required the Voskhod 1 crew to accept two huge inherent risks. First, the weight constraints caused by the third crew member meant they'd have to go up in shirtsleeves with no pressure suits. That meant that if the cabin sprung a leak at any time during the mission all three would die instantly. Second, there would be no room for ejection seats meaning that if the launch vehicle failed they would all unquestionably be killed. Finally, just to add a touch of absurdity to these unnecessary dangers, Khrushchev also decreed that the crew adopt strict caloric intake limits during training so that they could fit more easily into the smaller couches necessitated by squeezing three seats into a vehicle originally built to accommodate two men. The three cosmonauts who drew the short straws in this flying circus were named Vladimir Komorov, Konstantin Feoktistov and Boris Yegorov. As they rode the gantry elevator up to the top of the R-7 rocket to board Voskhod 1, it could not have been a confidence builder to gaze out over the steppes of Baikonur and see the landscape littered with the debris from several previous unsuccessful R-7 launches. Fortunately for the trio of cosmonauts, the Russians managed to get them into orbit for the one day flight. The final chapter of the crazy saga ended upon their return on October 13, 1964 with the cosmonauts being greeted by Russia's new leaders, Leonid Brezhnev and Alexei Kosygin. During the Voskhod's one day aloft, Khrushchev had been deposed and expelled from the Communist Party.

As THE CALENDAR TURNED to 1965, the race to the moon had not only become a national obsession in both the United States and the Soviet Union, it had sparked intense interest around the world as the two global superpowers with vastly different political ideologies had locked horns in a battle for supremacy in the heavens. In his address to Congress after Al Shepard's Mercury flight, John Kennedy had both upped the ante and created a finish line for the space race. If America was going to cross it first, Project Gemini had to succeed. With Shepard now grounded, the question on everyone's mind at NASA at that moment was who among the remaining astronauts would pick up the baton and command the first Gemini mission.

# Molly

**W**ith Slayton and Shepard both grounded and running the Astronaut Office, with Glenn seemingly bubble-wrapped by President Kennedy, with Carpenter's name sandblasted at the top of Chris Kraft's shitlist and with Gordo's penchant for infuriating the NASA brass, Grissom and Schirra had emerged as the only viable choices left from the original astronauts to command the first Gemini flight and, by God, Deke was going to have one of his Mercury brothers in command of that mission. After Liberty Bell 7's trip to the bottom of the Atlantic, time had worked in Gus's favor in a number of ways. First, the myriad of committees and boards of review convened by NASA after Liberty Bell sank had failed to uncover any malfeasance on Gus's part. In the meantime, for the reasons set forth above, several of his Mercury colleagues had regressed in the eyes of the NASA brass and a couple had bitten the dust entirely. While Wally's credentials for command were impeccable, Deke had no justifiable reason to move him ahead of Gus in the flight rotation and when one also considers the fact that Deke and Gus were test pilot colleagues in the Air Force while Wally was all Navy, Deke was probably not inclined to make any such change to begin with. So Gemini's first flight would be Gus's to command.

Virgil I. "Gus" Grissom was born on April 3, 1926, the eldest of Dennis and Cecile Grissom's four children. While growing up during the Great Depression, Gus delivered newspapers twice a day all year and picked peaches and cherries during the summer.

He also served as leader of the Honor Guard in his local Boy Scout troop. Despite his obviously strong work ethic, Gus didn't show much early interest in school, being described by his high school principal as "an average solid citizen." After a brief stint in the Army Air Corps, Gus married Betty Moore in July, 1945 and then would go on to earn a B.S. in mechanical engineering from Purdue University in 1950. Realizing his calling, Gus reenlisted in what was by then the U.S. Air Force. For flying 100 combat missions in Korea, Gus earned both the Air Medal with cluster and the Distinguished Flying Cross. After that, no one would ever again characterize Gus Grissom as being "average." A few years later, Gus landed at Edwards where he finished test pilot school in 1957 and shipped out to Wright-Patterson Air Base in Dayton where he specialized in testing new jet fighters. Having attained his career goal and in a job he loved, Gus was taken aback when he received a mysterious top secret order to report to Washington D.C. to test for what turned out to be NASA's Mercury program. Then, on April 3, 1959, NASA selected Gus as one of the first seven astronauts. After the Liberty Bell 7 saga unfolded, Gus's waiting game for Gemini had followed.

Aside from the circumstances that had sidelined some of his competitors from Mercury, another important factor in Gus's selection to command the first manned Gemini flight was his familiarity with the spacecraft's systems. In a move that certainly appeared to have been calculated and may well have been, Gus had cut bait and moved on from Mercury practically as soon as Liberty Bell 7 hit the ocean floor. This contrasted with Shepard who had continued to prowl around Mercury's perimeter as Cooper's backup for Faith 7 in turn politicking for either another even longer duration flight after Gordo's to close out the program or, when that looked unlikely to materialize, hoping somehow Gordo might screw up and get booted from Faith 7 so he could take his place. Gus, meanwhile, had already moved on to St. Louis and had begun working with the McDonnell team on the interior layout of what would become the Gemini spacecraft. Also, "From the program's outset Deke had charged Gus to ride herd on the Gemini design team and assure that the flight crew input and recommendations were transformed into actual hardware for the systems the astronauts, not the engineers, wanted."That would be necessary because Gemini would not employ the cannonball approach of the Mercury missions. Gemini would be a spacecraft that the astronauts could actually *fly*. The extent to which Gus's fingerprints were on the Gemini capsule soon became apparent. "The one ... thing that had happened to the Gemini craft and its interior fittings during their development was that they began to be fashioned around Gus Grissom—one of the smallest of the astronauts. Later, taller astronauts would have problems squeezing into the same space and using the same apparatus designed for Grissom's compact frame ... In fact, this became so evident that the astronauts began to call the Gemini spacecraft "the Gusmobile."

Of course, the issue remained as to who would join Grissom inside the Gusmobile on Gemini 3 and one thing was for damn sure—it wasn't going to be another of the Mercury astronauts. As any Mercury veteran flying second seat on any future spaceflight was not even remotely conceivable, Gus's crewmate was going to have to come from the New Nine. However, before that selection could even be made another issue had cropped up. On the two seat flight, the individual crew members would have to be given specific designations. Of course, the natural call signs would have been "pilot" and "co-pilot." But as Group 2 astronaut Jim Lovell pointed out, "No one in the astronaut corps wanted to be called a co-pilot. So NASA management, scratching their heads, finally came up with commander and pilot."

Eventually, Deke decided that Commander Grissom would be joined on Gemini's maiden flight by Pilot John W. Young. One of the New Nine, John was born on September 24, 1930 to William "Hugh" and Wanda Young. After growing up in Orlando, John would go on to Georgia Tech where he would join the Navy ROTC program and later graduate with a B.S. with highest honors in aeronautical engineering. Upon completing his NROTC training and passing his flight physical, Young had hoped to become a "brown shoe" or naval aviator. Instead, his commander assigned him to "black shoe" destroyer duty—a fact which Grissom delighted in never allowing him to forget. Young wasn't deterred and after a hitch aboard the USS Laws in the Korean War John was ordered to report to Pensacola for flying school on May 8, 1953. After years of gaining experience flying off aircraft carriers, Young was assigned in 1959 to the Naval ATC at Pax River. After distinguishing himself as a Navy test pilot, John got the call from Deke in early September, 1962 and he agreed to become a member of the New Nine. Then came the assignment to accompany Gus on GT-III.

With the mission objectives of the Mercury flights all being essentially the same: (a) survive liftoff; (b) hurtle up and down or around the Earth in a spacecraft with almost no maneuverability; (c) reenter the Earth's atmosphere without getting incinerated; and (d) land in one of the Earth's four oceans, a "next-man-up" approach in the flight rotation was perfectly feasible and, in fact, Carpenter had backed up Slayton, Schirra had backed up Carpenter and Cooper had backed up Schirra. However, with so many program objectives outlined over so many proposed flights, the next-man-up approach just wasn't going to work in Gemini. Accordingly, and reflecting Deke's belief that Wally Schirra was simply the best choice to replace Grissom if Gus were to be grounded or killed during training, Deke assigned Wally to be Gus's backup on GT-III although that meant that Wally could not be on the prime crew for Gemini IV given that the complex objectives and intricacies of that flight were entirely different from those of GT-III. As a result, Wally, as Gus's backup, had to train exclusively for GT-III which in turn meant that someone junior to Wally would get the command of GT-IV and go into space during Gemini before him. Later, when Deke assigned Wally to command the prime crew of Gemini VI after the GT-III flight, it began a Slayton tradition that a backup crew would skip two missions and then become the prime crew of the third. It was an unwritten rule from which Deke would rarely deviate throughout the duration of the Gemini program except in the case of astronaut malfeasance or some sort of calamity within the program.

Unfortunately, the second part of that equation would become an all too common occurrence in the future.

Of course, since a backup was required for Gus, one would also be required for Young. For that task, Deke chose Young's fellow New Niner, Thomas P. "Tom" Stafford. Tom had actually been chosen to join Big Al on the prime crew for the first Gemini flight but, after Shepard developed Meniere's, Tom found himself on the outside looking in due to Deke's reluctance to break up or mix and match crewmen once missions had been assigned. Even with the gut punch, Stafford would still end up being the fifth of the New Nine selected to go up following after Young, McDivitt, White and Conrad. Once given his chance, Stafford would go on to prove himself to be one of NASA's steadiest and most capable astronauts.

Once crew selection was complete and training began, it was time for the GT-III commander to continue a tradition going back to Shepard's Freedom 7—that of naming the spacecraft. Charged with the task, Grissom came up with what later was described as a "devilish notion." Having never forgotten how many people at NASA and particularly in the press had never let him forget the sinking of Liberty Bell 7, Gus decided to name the spacecraft "Molly Brown" which he borrowed from "The Unsinkable Molly Brown," a hit Broadway show and movie about the 1912 maritime heroine. The NASA brass, being the NASA brass, balked at the cheekiness of Gus's selection and asked him if he had a second choice. When Gus replied, "uh ... Titanic," the brass decided that maybe Molly Brown wasn't so bad after all. Still, Gus's choice of Molly Brown, coming on the heels of Gordo's "Faith 7," had sufficiently chapped NASA's collective ass to the point that an order came down from Headquarters decreeing that no future NASA spacecraft would have names, only mission designations.

Of course the spacecraft, regardless of what they ended up calling it, was going to require ground control. That, in turn, would require a flight director and, as had been the case for every Mercury mission, the prime flight director for GT-III would be the brilliant and charismatic Christopher Columbus Kraft, Jr.. Born February 28, 1924 in the tidewater town of Phoebus, Virginia,

Kraft would earn a B.S. in aeronautical engineering from Virginia Tech in 1944. Shortly thereafter, he accepted a position with the National Advisory Committee for Aeronautics (NACA) which would eventually be absorbed into NASA in 1958. While working at NACA, Kraft would become acquainted with Robert R. "Bob" Gilruth, then head of research at NACA, a man for whom Kraft would develop sincere admiration and who would be a close friend and mentor for the next three decades. Following the formation of NASA, it was Gilruth who invited Kraft to join the Space Task Group (STG) on November 5, 1958 and Kraft accepted. The STG was composed of 35 engineers whose job it was to figure out how to put a man into space and, ideally, bring him back down alive. As Kraft would say, "The job ahead had never been done before. We would learn by doing. So we got started."

The program that the STG created came to be known as Project Mercury. One of the earliest and most fundamental lessons that the STG learned was the enormous difference between flying airplanes and flying into space. Of course, the vehicles involved would be completely different but there was a lot more to the equation than spacecraft design and booster development. In spaceflight, ways had to be invented to track and then recover the vehicle and to communicate with its occupant while the vehicle was outside the Earth's atmosphere. Also, the systems inside the vehicle had to be continually monitored by support personnel on the ground. The obvious problem was that in 1959 humankind had yet to develop the capability to do any of those things and each of them would have to be invented on the fly. And not only that. All of that new technology would have to be harnessed and brought under the concurrent control of one facility. The overall concept would come to be characterized as flight control from the ground. That, in turn, would give rise to what would become known as the Mercury Control Center—and the facility and its layout were each the brainchild of Chris Kraft. Since Kraft had essentially designed the Mercury control facility, it was only logical that Gilruth would choose Kraft to be the Mercury Flight Director, charged with personally overseeing all of the communications circuits (or "loops" as they came to be known) between every flight controller's console. It was a role Kraft would hold exclusively until Faith 7 when the length of Gordo's mission necessitated a backup for Kraft.

Of course, with technological advances being made so rapidly, Mercury Control was almost obsolete before it became operational. With the longer and exceedingly more complex missions to come, a newer, larger and much more advanced facility would be required for the Gemini flights and, particularly, the lunar exploration missions of Apollo on down the line. Gilruth would charge Kraft with the primary responsibility for designing and overseeing the construction of that facility as well. But for Gemini 3, good old Mercury Control would have one last hurrah at the Cape before the whole flight control circus packed up and moved to its permanent home in Houston.

Finally, with both spacecraft and booster man–rated, it was time for the NASA brass to decide exactly what they wanted Gemini 3 to accomplish. NASA vernacular for this statement of purpose was the "Mission Objectives" and for the flight of Gemini 3 they would be relatively straightforward. With Mercury behind them, the administrators and flight control team felt confident that they could get the Gemini spacecraft off the launchpad, into orbit and back down again. In Mercury, that had been enough. Now that was no longer the case. In Gemini, just surviving the journey into space wasn't going to move the program and the country forward. Accordingly, it was time for the next step on the journey to the moon.

Gemini 3 was what test pilots call a "shakedown" flight designed to examine the spacecraft's internal systems through liftoff, orbit insertion, orbital flight and reentry. If all went as planned, NASA could proceed with future missions confident that the Gemini capsule was spaceworthy. That had to be done. However, the primary goal of the flight, if Grissom and Young could pull it off, was to be the use of the spacecraft's Orbital Attitude and Maneuver System (called "OAMS" in Mission Control) to determine if it was possible for the spacecraft's flight path to be altered manually by the astronauts while in orbit using an onboard computer and thrusters spread about on the exterior of spacecraft. Developing the capability was not merely crucial but essential in order for one spacecraft to fly in tandem with another in space. Now that Lunar Orbit Rendezvous (LOR) had been selected as the mode for the lunar missions, orbital rendezvous had to be accomplished or LOR would fail and so would NASA's quest to be first to land a man on the lunar surface and bring him back to Earth alive. In order for rendezvous to ultimately be achieved, Gemini 3 first had to demonstrate that precise spacecraft maneuvers in Earth orbit were possible. Finally, NASA had tacked on three additional experiments. The first was designed to measure the effects of exposure to radiation in space on human blood cells. The second one involved the use of fertilized sea urchin eggs to study the effects of microgravity on cell structure and the final one required Gemini 3 to inject water into the ionized plasma caused by reentry in an attempt to shorten or eliminate the ground to air radio blackout caused by the ionization.

With the mission checklist established, Gus and John hit the flight line shortly after 5:00 a.m. on March 23, 1965 and were inside the ship with the hatch sealed at half past seven. At 9:24 a.m., down below inside the Titan II, valves opened causing the Aerozin 50 to hit the nitrogen tetroxide and the Gemini program was underway. Capcom Gordon Cooper marked the historic moment with an enthusiastic "You're on your way, Molly Brown" which was a nice heads-up because although the engine ignition was audible Gemini 3's liftoff was so smooth that Young had to glance at the mission clock on the instrument panel just to assure himself that they had left the pad. John did, however, get quite a start about 2½ minutes later at staging. When the Titan's second stage ignited while the first stage was still attached, it created what came to be known as the "fire in the hole" effect during which the spacecraft was engulfed by a yellow-orange flame streaking past it. Thankfully the phenomenon was only momentary as the Titan's second stage with its additional 100,000 pounds of thrust had soon had lifted Molly Brown up past the fireball and into the blackness of space. Five and a half minutes after liftoff, the second stage shut down and Gus kicked the spacecraft into orbit with a blast from the aft thrusters. When the dust had settled, Gus and John found themselves in an elliptical orbit of 87 by 125 miles above the Earth.

Approximately twenty-four minutes after liftoff, Young noticed that the cabin pressure gauge read zero prompting him and a startled Grissom to quickly lower their pressure suit helmet visors. It turned out that the malfunction was in the instrument panel's power supply and Young switched to a secondary system which alleviated the problem. Then, after having a go at the food, and the radiation and sea urchin egg experiments, it was time for Gemini 3 to make some history. Having received word from Carnavon Capcom Pete Conrad that they were go for a second orbit, the crew initiated the first OAMS burn with Grissom calling out "Mark!" at 1:33:00 Mission Elapsed Time (MET). A second later, Young stated "Okay, they appear to be firing good." At 1:34:18, Texas Capcom confirmed maneuver complete. Three seconds later, Young stated, "That burn was one minute and fourteen seconds by our watches." At 1:50:32, Canary Capcom confirmed, "After your burn, your orbit is 85.6, 92.6." One minute and fourteen seconds. That's all it took to complete the maneuver which changed Gemini 3's elliptical orbit around the Earth to one that was damn near circular. But in that brief span of time, Grissom and Young had done far more than merely make Gemini 3 the first spacecraft to ever have its orbit manually reconfigured by an astronaut in flight. They'd also altered the trajectory of the space race.

The second firing of the OAMS system which came approximately 45 minutes later in the mission was a maneuver of the utmost importance as well, as it would demonstrate that the Gemini spacecraft could by firing of the thrusters in measured bursts change the angle of the orbit ("the orbital plane" they called it) relative to the Earth below. This essentially proved that the Gemini spacecraft could move laterally in space which was just as important for rendezvous capability as the ability to raise or lower the spacecraft's orbit. The third and final test of the OAMS system required Grissom to perform a 2½ minute burn that dropped

Molly Brown into a seventy two kilometer "fail-safe" orbit which would precipitate a reentry even if the reentry control system (RCS) retro-rockets failed to fire.

Fortunately for everyone involved, the retros did fire. At 4:32:36 Young called adapter separation. At 4:33:13 Rose Knot Victor Capcom counted from ten down to retrofire which Gus confirmed as "all retros fired normally" 21 seconds later. Despite the attempt to add moisture to the ionization, there was still a five minute blackout until the ground started picking up chatter from Young. At 4:46:48 Gus confirmed that the drogue was out. A couple minutes later, after Gus called the main chute stable, Young said something about the descent being "the roughest of the bunch." It turned out that when the main chute was deployed both astronauts helmets (which they had yet to remove from their heads) slammed into the spacecraft's windshields. Young reported the spacecraft was still showing 200 feet altitude when they hit the water at 4:52:31.

The combination of excessive lift from the Titan during launch, Gus popping the thrusters too hard at second stage cutoff and perhaps even the residuals of one or more of the OAMS tests caused Gemini 3 to undershoot the recovery forces by approximately 50 miles. At splashdown, the ship was inverted until Gus realized the chutes were still attached and dragging the capsule through the water. Gus then jettisoned the chutes and the ship stabilized. Still, it was no picnic. Young was beginning to appreciate his black shoe days on the Laws as he was somehow able to hold it together although he later commented that Molly Brown "was no boat." Poor Gus, on the other hand, vomited his guts out. Still, there was no way in hell that this flight was going to end up being "Liberty Bell 7: The Sequel." Gus literally would have died inside Molly Brown before he allowed it to sink with him on the outside. When the recovery forces finally secured a flotation collar on the ship, Gus dragged himself out of the hatch and into a life raft. But not before Gemini 3 was an unqualified success and this time, by God, he'd brought the ship back intact. And everyone in the press could stick that "squirmin' hatchblower" nonsense where the Good Lord intended all such things to be stuck.

Splashdown and recovery should have been the end of the Gemini 3 story but, regrettably, it wasn't. For no complete recounting of the mission can be told without some mention of "The Sandwich." Fortunately for Gus and John, the events in question transpired before 1973 or the entire matter undoubtedly would have ended up being forever known as "Sandwichgate." The whole thing started when Wally Schirra, notorious for his practical jokes and in typical Schirra fashion, thrust a wrapped-up corned beef sandwich from a Cocoa Beach deli into Young's hand out on Pad 19 just as he and Gus were about to be shoehorned into the spacecraft. Being junior to Schirra, John couldn't exactly toss it back at Wally and tell him to shove off so he took it and jammed it into one of the pockets of his spacesuit. That precipitated this surreal onboard conversation:

MET: 1:52:26: Gus: What is that?

1:52:27: Young: Corn beef sandwich.

1:52:28: Gus: Where did that come from?

1:52:30: Young: I brought it with me. Let's see how it tastes. Smells, doesn't it?

1:52:41: Gus: Yes, it's breaking up. I'm going to stick it in my pocket.

1:52:49: Young: It was a thought anyway.

1:52:51: Gus: Yep.

1:52:52: Young: Not a very good one.

Yeah, John, not a very good one. Years later, Young would wryly comment that Gus had chastised him with "What, you brought a corned beef sandwich into space and forgot the damn mustard?" If only the aftermath of the situation had been that lighthearted. Because when word of the corned beef sandwich incident got out all kinds of people went bonkers. The NASA brass whined that the crumbs from the sandwich could've gotten behind the control panel and shorted out God–knows-what. The NASA doctors, always seemingly in search of something to complain about, groused that by eating part of an unauthorized sandwich Grissom and Young had negated any useful data that could have been gleaned from the crew's consumption of the carefully packaged and precisely rationed onboard food. And then, of course, came the outcry of the congressmen. One of them, conveniently overlooking the fact that Gus and John had just put their asses on the line flying a flawless mission for his country, even suggested that both astronauts should either be grounded or dismissed from NASA altogether. Although justifiably ignored, his statement was demonstrative proof that U.S. congressmen of Gemini's era were the same sort of pious, pontificating charlatans that inhabit our nation's Capital today. Thankfully, the whole mess eventually blew over.

OF COURSE, HISTORICAL EVENTS never happen in a vacuum and such was the case with Gemini 3. Only five days before Gus and John were scheduled for liftoff, the Russians once again poked a sharp stick into the eye of their decadent capitalist counterparts. On March 18, 1965, word began to make its way West that not only had the Soviets successfully launched and recovered Voskhod 2 but also that during the mission cosmonaut Alexei Leonov had actually ventured outside the capsule and successfully completed the world's first "spacewalk." The part that they didn't bother sharing with the rest of the world was that while outside Leonov's spacesuit had inflated like a balloon transforming him into something resembling a cosmic Stay-Puft Marshmallow Man. That, in turn, had caused him to get stuck like a cork in a bottle in the tunnel-like airlock attached to the Voskhod when he tried to reenter the vehicle. This caused Leonov, a superb cosmonaut, to have to improvise. With his oxygen running low and his life hanging in the balance, Leonov sufficiently depressurized his suit while stuck in the airlock to force his way back down inside the tunnel and into the Voskhod. Then, to add insult to injury, the next day a systems failure forced mission commander Pavel Belyayev to fly a manual reentry which resulted in a one thousand mile overshoot of the planned recovery zone. The flight ended with Voskhod 2 wedged in the top of a stand of fir trees in a forest near the Urals. Stuck there overnight awaiting rescue, Leonov and Belyayev damn near froze to death. The Soviets, while blaring the news of Leonov's historic feat and declaring it a Russian triumph on par with that of Gagarin, conveniently forgot to mention that he had nearly been killed in the airlock or that socialism's newest golden boys had transformed the Mother Country's mighty Voskhod into a fucking treehouse. Khrushchev may have been banished into oblivion but the Soviet Union was still the Soviet Union.

CHAPTER 2

# The Boy Scout Takes a Walk

O ne of the more common assumptions about the flight plan for Gemini IV was that what would eventually become its primary mission objective, that of having an astronaut float free outside the spacecraft while attached to a life support tether (or "going EVA"), was a direct American response to Leonov's extravehicular activity on Voskhod 2. While that Soviet feat certainly had a substantial impact on the decision by NASA to go EVA on Gemini IV, the full story is a bit more nuanced than that. As Deke said, "I figured to handpick the crews for the first four Gemini missions, since they had unique requirements, and treat the last six as more or less identical. In talking things over with some of the guys, I knew, for example, that Wally wasn't eager to fly a long-duration mission but figured that he'd do a good job on rendezvous. Al had been backup on the last Mercury and was more or less in line for the first Gemini; He was also the most capable pilot we had. Gus had dug in on the Gemini systems and would be a good candidate for a long-duration flight; Gordo might work in here too.

I also wanted to give someone from the 1962 group an early chance at command. So in my first pass at a long-term plan, the early Gemini missions slots were taken like this:

GT-3    (First Mission) Shepard

GT-4    (Seven days)    1962 Astronaut

GT-5    (Rendezvous)    Schirra

GT-6    (Fourteen days) Grissom …"

So, according to Deke's assessment of NASA's immediate plans, not only was the original GT-IV flight supposed to be a seven day duration mission, apparently there was no intention of having any sort of EVA on any flight until at least Gemini VII. Further, as events played themselves out, there were a myriad of factors that had nothing to do with the Russians or Leonov's achievement that caused a significant scrambling of the various Gemini mission objectives—not to mention the Gemini crews—that Deke had envisioned for the first four flights as they were laid out in early 1964.

As to the specific factors impacting Gemini IV, NASA had "decided to use a fuel cell, developed by the General Electric Co., on longer missions. Light, simple in design and well-suited to the requirements of Gemini, the fuel cell used hydrogen and oxygen in a reaction that produced both water and heat. The cell design used a solid ion-exchanging membrane, which chemically bonded electrolyte and water instead of diffusing gases into liquid electrolyte, as featured in other designs of cells. Using a separate stream of coolant, the water produced at the cell was condensed and removed through a series of wicks, enabling the reaction to continue at a constant rate. This in turn used very little of the cell's own power, rendering it more efficient and simpler in design. Two groups of fuel cells could each provide 1,000W, which was sufficient for the spacecraft's total electrical needs. As a by-product, water was produced for drinking and spacecraft cooling." Nifty, huh? The problem was that these proposed fuel cells were not going to be ready in time for Gemini IV. That meant that the spacecraft would have to be powered by batteries which had no regenerative capability. That, in turn, meant the mission could last no longer than four days due to the size constraints of the Gemini spacecraft. Although that in itself was three times longer than Gordo had flown during Faith 7, it was no doubt engrained at NASA that the Soviets had flown Nicolayev for 64 orbits on a four day mission over two years ago. Although a proposal for a limited, perhaps "stand-up" EVA (during which the pilot would open the hatch and stand up in his seat without fully egressing the spacecraft) had been floated—without generating much enthusiasm—as a possible mission objective for Gemini IV, now that the seven day duration flight (with Soviet–record breaking potential) was off the table, NASA management began to warm to the possibility of raising the stakes and going for a full-blown EVA on Gemini IV. As Chris Kraft explained, "The major accomplishment of our three revolution Gemini 3 flight, maneuvering in space, was now fact, not theory. But it looked puny to politicians and even to some reporters, when compared to what the Russians had done with Alexei Leonov's spacewalk. Inside NASA, we understood that spacecraft needed maneuvering capability and that the Russian ships had none. But they got headlines anyway. Extravehicular activity was on Gemini's agenda. Bob Gilruth asked the question in a meeting with his senior staff: 'With the Gemini IV flight plan in total disarray anyway, should we include EVA in the rewrite?'"

As Kraft would point out, if Gilruth's question was to be answered affirmatively then a whole bunch of hardware was going to have to be tested and man-rated in a hurry. First, it had to be proven that the Gemini spacecraft's hatches could be opened and closed in space. Second, pressurized spacesuits had to be able to withstand testing in a vacuum. Third, a life-sustaining umbilical cord carrying oxygen and communications equipment from the spacecraft had to be developed along with an emergency cannister of oxygen to be strapped to the astronaut's chest in case the tether failed. Finally, to top it all off, NASA wanted to develop a hand-held "zip gun" that used nitrogen gas to propel the space-walker and which would allow him to perform controlled maneuvers around the spacecraft and use it to essentially one-up Leonov, who'd merely gotten out and floated around.

Once the hardware had been tested and approved, the NASA brass went all in and a full-blown outside-the-spacecraft EVA was added to the flight plan of Gemini IV. Upon accepting that challenge, Kraft turned to a trusted subordinate to put together a clandestine training schedule to take the theoretical EVA plan and turn it into reality. Kraft's choice in that regard would have a far greater impact on the future of the American space program than the decision to go EVA on Gemini IV. For it marked the arrival on the Mission Control scene of a reddish-orange haired crewcut force of nature named Eugene F. "Gene" Kranz. A former Air Force (not a Marine, dammit) pilot, Kranz had made his way to the Space Task Group at Langley in October, 1960. It was there that he would first encounter Chris Kraft. Mentored by Kraft as Kraft had been mentored by Gilruth, it was a case of greatness begetting greatness begetting greatness. Because he would end up on console as the prime flight director for the first moon landing as well as Jim Lovell's "Houston, we have a problem" call made iconic by Ron Howard's Apollo 13 movie, Kranz's fame would eventually surpass even that of Kraft who was a household name himself in 1960s' America. But, for now, Gene was just another damned rookie, he had a job to do and he would have to prove himself to Kraft and the rest of Mission Control. As to Kranz's current assignment, Kraft was blunt when telling Gene in late March, 1965, "We are going to do an EVA if we can get the equipment ready in June. I want you to write the rules and put together the data package we will need to carry out the mission." By essentially working double-shifts for the next two months, Kranz succeeded splendidly in completing the daunting task which Kraft had assigned him. For Gene Kranz, as it would always be throughout his NASA career, failure was not an option.

While they were at it, NASA's administrators, who'd once worried about rushing into an EVA before the program was prepared for it, decided to double down on Gemini IV and add yet another complex mission objective. Since the rendezvous target vehicle for many of the Gemini program's later objectives, the Agena rocket, was nowhere near ready for flight, the NASA brass decided to have Gemini IV attempt to rendezvous with the second stage of the Titan booster shortly after Sustainer Engine Cut-Off (SECO) and spacecraft separation had been achieved. So, what had begun as a seven day fly-around with some photography and science experiments had now morphed into a complex four day duration/ EVA flight with an untested rendezvous maneuver thrown in for good measure. It was going to take one hell of a crew to pull it all off. Deke knew exactly who he wanted that crew to be.

Staying true to his plan to name a New Nine astronaut to command Gemini IV, Deke selected James Alton "Jim" McDivitt to fill that role. McDivitt was born on June 10, 1929 in Chicago and his family later relocated to Kalamazoo, Michigan where Jim graduated from Central High School. After graduating from Michigan's Jackson Junior College in June of 1950, McDivitt entered the Air Force as an aviation cadet in January, 1951 and earned his pilot's wings and a commission in May of that year. In late 1951, he shipped out to Korea and flew the required 100 combat missions and then stayed on and volunteered for 45 more, flying both the Lockheed F-80 and North American F-86 Sabre during his hitch. For his service in Korea, McDivitt was awarded the Air Force Distinguished Service Medal with oak leaf cluster, the Distinguished Flying Cross with three oak leaf clusters and the Air Medal with four oak leaf clusters. Jim then went on to graduate first in his class while earning a B.S. in aeronautical engineering from the University of Michigan in 1959. Before being selected as a member of the New Nine in September, 1962, Jim graduated from the USAF Experimental Test Pilot School and had served as a test pilot at Edwards.

Despite his sparking résumé and the obvious fact that he'd done something to set himself apart (at least in Slayton's eyes) and had moved to the top of the New Nine pecking order—which could have stirred some jealously among his colleagues—it seemed that no one, inside the astronaut corps or out, had anything bad to say about Jim McDivitt. Had he been a character in a 1940s movie, Jim would've been the fella that all the dames referred to as "a swell guy." Unfailingly affable and forthright, while studying at the University of Michigan, Jim had met and forged a close friendship with another like–minded straight arrow. That guy's name was Edward Higgins White II.

Ed White was born in San Antonio on November 14, 1930 and, although his family moved to Hawaii while he was still in his crib, Ed always considered himself a Texan. The son of a U.S. Army aviator, Ed followed in his father's footsteps by first securing an appointment to the U.S. Military Academy and then graduating from West Point in 1952. Ed then served as a fighter pilot in Germany until 1957 when the Air Force decided to send him to the University of Michigan where he wound up living down the street from McDivitt. Given their closeness in age (attending college in their late twenties) and their shared military backgrounds, it was only natural that the two former fighter pilots would gravitate toward one another and away from their much younger fellow students. In fact, McDivitt, who was vacillating over his next career move while at Michigan, would later credit White with planting the test pilot idea in his head and both would go on to graduate from EFTS class 59-C at Edwards. From there, White was assigned to Wright-Patterson as a test pilot with the Aeronautical Systems Division. Later, after they'd been selected to the New Nine, McDivitt walked into a room at the Pentagon for a NASA initial selection interview when he came face to face with his best friend. "I knew you'd be here." White said to McDivitt. Jim replied, "I knew you'd be here, too." As Slayton would later reveal in setting forth his crew-selection criteria, "I would try to match people in a crew based on individual talents and, when possible, personal compatibility." Employing that standard, pairing White with McDivitt was practically inevitable. These two guys weren't just fighter jocks, they were patriots.

White was also widely considered to be the best athlete in the astronaut corps. It was no small feat considering the competition and was a definite factor in the decision to have him go EVA on Gemini IV. One warm evening in Houston both Ed's character and his athleticism were put to the test under the most extreme circumstances. Upon arriving in Houston, Ed and his wife Pat had settled next to another New Nine astronaut household headed by Neil and Janet Armstrong. Sleeping with their bedroom window open because of the heat, Ed heard a commotion next door and what was clearly Janet Armstrong's voice in some sort of distress. Upon stepping outside to investigate, it immediately became apparent that the Armstrong home was on fire. Separating the two houses was a six foot high wooden backyard fence. Knowing that the Armstrongs' two young boys were inside the home, Ed went straight for the fence and, as Janet Armstrong would later attest, leapt it. Only Ed didn't barrel-roll it like a high jumper of the era but rather tucked his legs under him and swung himself by the arms over the top. Then, Ed grabbed a hose to attempt to douse the fire passing it to Janet only when Neil handed his 10 month old son out to Ed so that Neil could go back inside and save his other son. It was a textbook example of Ed simply being Ed. When other people ran away from the fire, Ed White ran to it. Group 3 astronaut Eugene Cernan wasn't overstating the point in later years when he said, "Ed White was probably the closest thing we had to a Boy Scout in the astronaut corps."

Before Gemini IV would go aloft, there had been some significant changes in flight control operations—foremost among them the shifting of the locale of the nerve center of all future missions from the Mercury Control Center at the Cape to the newly minted Mission Operations Control Room (MOCR— pronounced MO—ker) in Houston. The public would come to refer to MOCR more commonly as Mission Control. In truth, flight operations had outgrown Mercury Control even before the Mercury program had ended. One of the primary reasons was the growing realization that as NASA's missions became longer and their objectives grew more complex, there was going to be an urgent need for more sophisticated hardware to track the spacecraft in orbit. Also, communications between Kraft and his flight controllers and between the controllers themselves could only generously be described as chaotic employing a network of runners physically carrying written dispatches between parties to their various consoles. This, in turn, would result in piles of spent paper messages being discarded on the floor around the controllers' work stations and particularly around the Flight Director's console.

In seeking input into the design and construction of the new mission control facility as well as who ought to be contracted to build it, NASA Chief Administrator James "Jim" Webb quite predictably turned to Chris Kraft. As Kraft stated, "While Mercury was still only halfway finished, I had to be closely involved with planning our new Control Center in Houston. We divided the work into two pieces, a state-of-the-art Real-Time Computer Complex (RTCC) and then two separate, but identical mission control rooms. We assumed that we'd be flying missions so closely together that one room would be dedicated to the current mission and the other to the upcoming mission." Then, when Webb asked Kraft to recommend contractors for building the Mission Control rooms and the computer systems for them, Kraft recommended Philco for the former and IBM for the latter. In short order Webb selected both Philco and IBM for the respective jobs.

When the work down at Houston was completed, mission operations was housed in Building 30 of the Space Center Complex. For the Gemini missions the interior design of the MOCR featured three ascending rows of consoles providing work stations for the Flight Director and each individual flight controller. The first row, which would come to be known as "The Trench" provided support for the Flight Dynamics Officers (FIDO), Booster Systems Engineer (Booster), as well as the assistant FIDO and an experiments officer. As Kraft Red Team member John Aaron described The Trench, "Their's was a world of orbital mechanics." In essence, The Trench collectively would keep track of the spacecraft's attitude and trajectory in orbit. The second row was home to the Vehicle Systems Engineer (Systems), Guidance Officer (Guido) as well as the Capcom and Flight Surgeon. Together, the second row guys were charged with monitoring everything going on inside the spacecraft during a mission. Finally, in the third row at the top of the pyramid, sat the Flight Director. To add texture to that antiseptic description, Kranz provided these more human details of the environment he and his colleagues experienced once they stepped onto the control room floor. "As they worked, they smoked and soon the usual pall of blue smoke hung in the air over the consoles. Stale cigarette butts, cold coffee and day-old pizza made up the scent of Mission Control … Mission Control was windowless. No clock referenced us to local time in Houston. Greenwich mean time, the local time in England, synchronized us to our stations around the world. Then as now, every action, both in the spacecraft and on the ground, worked to time that started ticking after liftoff—Mission Elapsed Time (MET). Our bodies were the only laggards, responding to the need for food and rest on a schedule corresponding to a sun we couldn't see."

Adding to the disorientation problem for the flight control team, of course, was that once the spacecraft was aloft, it had to be continuously monitored in case some mission critical event took place which would require the vehicle to be brought down immediately. This meant that Chris Kraft could no longer handle all of the Flight Director's duties himself. Like it or not, Kraft was going to have to delegate some of that potential mission critical responsibility and it was determined that the Gemini IV mission would run three eight hour shifts. The Red Team, led by Kraft himself, would be on console for the EVA, the booster rendezvous attempt and most of the other high profile mission objectives (i.e. executing the flight plan). Kranz's White Team would then put the crew to sleep and analyze the spacecraft's systems and then check the status of consumables—oxygen, water and food foremost among them. John Hodge's Blue Team, called the planning shift, would then review Kranz's team's data, revise the flight plan, if necessary, then wake up the crew and brief them on the day's flight plan before handing the crew back off to Kraft and his guys. As a precautionary measure, no doubt due in part to this being the maiden voyage for the Houston facilities, Kraft sent Flight Director Glynn Lunney and his Black team to Mercury Control at the Cape to back up all three shifts in the event of a major systems failure in the new MOCR.

With all the pieces now in place in Houston, it was time to send Gemini IV into space. On June 3, 1965, McDivitt and White were awakened at 4:10 a.m. and had the traditional prelaunch steak and eggs breakfast. They were then driven to Pad 16 for the suiting-up process at the pre-flight ready room. From there, they rode the transfer van to Pad 19 and at 7:07 a.m., they ascended the gantry elevator up to the eleventh level where their spacecraft awaited. By T minus 100 minutes, they were strapped down inside the ship.

Given NASA's blissful ignorance where the complexities of rendezvous were concerned, the flight plan for Gemini IV was probably overly ambitious given the technical realities of early 1965. Looking back at it now with the benefit of hindsight, it is clear that it bordered on recklessness. Essentially, the mission plan called for McDivitt, a rookie commander making his first spaceflight, to shake off the effects of experiencing his first rocket launch into space, lock in at SECO just five minutes into the flight, then turn the spacecraft around and use thruster control to rendezvous with the second stage of the Titan. Then, Jim would perform a series of stationkeeping maneuvers to keep the booster in close proximity while White prepared for and then performed the first–ever American EVA which would include the requirement of Jim taking photographs of Ed spacewalking with the booster in the background. Although NASA and the crew obviously didn't realize it at the time, it would have taken a miracle for two rookies to pull all that off without any sort of glitch. That would become apparent within minutes after the launch of Gemini IV.

Al Shepard, launch Capcom at the Cape, called ignition and liftoff at 10:16 a.m. Then, for the first time in the history of American spaceflight, control of the mission was handed off to Houston from the Cape as soon as the Titan's engines cleared the top of the launch tower. McDivitt called out, "We're on our way, buddy" at :02, followed by "Good staging" at 2:34 and "SECO" at 5:34. McDivitt had turned around sufficiently to call "I got the old second stage" at 7:14 and Gus Grissom, acting as Houston Capcom, confirmed orbit to McDivitt less than a minute later. Now, it was time for McDivitt to attempt to rendezvous with the booster. Over the Canary Islands, McDivitt called at 18:31, "I have it sighted at this time. It's directly below me about 400 or 500 feet. I'm going to thrust down." *Going to thrust down.* Predictably, McDivitt's fighter pilot instincts had kicked in. With the booster below him, McDivitt figured he could lock on to it, increase his rate of acceleration and simply run it down. Had Jim been chasing the booster within the confines of the Earth's atmosphere that might have worked. Deke best described what happened next,

"Jim tried thrusting toward it and only managed to get farther away. (Basic orbital mechanics. Thrust toward something and you increase your velocity, which actually puts you in a higher orbit... where you will be going slower than you were when you fired your thrusters to increase your speed. It's a hard thing to learn since it's kind of backward from anything you know as a pilot.)" Jim was like a guy running a footrace in which he was behind his competitor and ran harder to catch up only to find himself—for reasons he did not yet fully comprehend—falling farther and farther behind. At just over 45 minutes into the flight, McDivitt called that he was now "probably a half a mile or so" away from the booster. At 1:28:00, McDivitt noted that he was burning through quite a lot of fuel just to keep the booster in sight. A minute and a half later, McDivitt was at the end of his rope, stating that he and Ed, "have to get a resolution right away whether you want me to really make a major effort to close this last thing or to save the fuel." In Houston, Kraft turned to Grissom and said "Give it up ... tell him to save the fuel." Gus sent up the call at 1:30:51. Thus ended— unceremoniously and unsuccessfully—America's first attempt at a rendezvous in space. Deke demonstrated his capacity for under- statement when he later observed, "Frankly, it wasn't an operation that had been too well thought out ...". Roger that.

With the booster rendezvous fiasco now thankfully in their rearview mirror, Jim and Ed could now devote their attention to their primary mission objective. That meant getting suited up (a more arduous task for Ed, obviously, since he was doing the EVA) so that they could begin cabin depressurization for hatch opening. Capcom Grissom made it official at 1:33:22 calling up, "We're giving you a go for your EVA at this time."

As to EVA preparation, "White put the zip gun together, while McDivitt read off a list of things for him to do. White pulled out the umbilical package and mounted suit connectors for the tether and the emergency oxygen chest pack." But problems were begin- ning to take shape. While helping Jim with all the hullaballoo surrounding the attempted rendezvous with the booster, Ed had had little time to devote to the EVA preparation checklist. Now he was trying to rush through it in time to make the scheduled attempt during Gemini IV's second orbit. It was at that point that McDivitt noticed that his friend was beginning to look "tired and hot." At 2:28:46 McDivitt, while not offering any commentary on Ed's condition, advised Carnavon that they were "running a little late and we might not be ready." Jim called it over Hawaii at 2:50:54 stating, "Next pass around. I don't think we want to try it." Accordingly, the EVA had been postponed until Gemini IV's third orbit.

At 4:07:24, McDivitt called down that the hatch lock was open. Three minutes later, White remarked that he and Jim were "in a vacuum now" meaning that cabin depressurization was complete. Then at 4:14:22 over Carnavon, White ominously reported that his hatch was "not moving a bit." After a somewhat protracted struggle, McDivitt called down to Hawaii at 4:26:07 that Ed "has the hatch open. He's standing in the seat." Then, four minutes later, Ed reported, "I'm separating from the spacecraft at this time." At 4:30:26 Ed advised, "My feet are out" and, just like that, America had its first human satellite. Twelve seconds later, Jim added, "He's floating free."

The one aspect of Leonov's EVA that the NASA team was determined to better was that Leonov, once free of the Voskhod, had seemed to just tumble around outside the ship. In order to top that, NASA devised a way to enable Ed to actually control his movements relative to the spacecraft. That's where the Hand Held Maneuvering Unit (HHMU) or "zip-gun" as it had come to be known came into play. In fact, the device was so small and carried so little fuel that White quickly exhausted it but apparently it was fun while it lasted with Ed proclaiming, "I feel like a million dollars" at 4:32:16. Three minutes later, White described himself as having the "greatest experience" and, more importantly, "absolutely no disorientation associated with it," demonstrating that the dizziness Leonov had reported while outside Voskhod 2 was not caused by the EVA itself. Perhaps it was simply a sign that the American was physically superior to the Russian, no? In any event, by 4:42:31, the astronauts were relaxed enough to engage in the following exchange: McDivitt: "You smeared up my windshield you dirty dog!" To which White replied: "Hand me out a Kleenex."

Down in Mission Control, Chris Kraft wasn't feeling quite as high-spirited as his crew. A design feature (Kraft probably would have called it a design flaw) of the spacecraft was that it locked Mission Control out of the communications loop once the onboard EVA comm system between McDivitt and White had been engaged. Because that system had worked to perfection, Kraft could hear the two crewmates yapping away at each other with no way to cut in and warn them that they were about to run out of daylight. With the zip gun's fuel exhausted, White had now resorted to pulling on the tether to maneuver (let that one sink in for a second) along with trying to jam the tips of his slick-soled boots into the corrugation of the spacecraft's exterior—and he still had to make it back inside. With the top of Kraft's head about ready to blow off, McDivitt finally flipped the comm switch to let Houston back in the loop, asking "Gus, this is Jim. Got any message for us?" The answer came up not from Grissom but from Kraft who, for the first (and, as it would turn out, only) time in his long and distinguished career, used his switch to override the Capcom, and barked into his microphone, "Tell him to get back in!". After a couple minutes' worth of recalcitrance on White's part, McDivitt demanded at 4:48:02, "Ed, come on in here." Seconds later, White, like a youngster called into supper by his mother while standing at home plate with a bat in his hands uttered, "This is the saddest moment of my life." McDivitt replied that he'd "find a sadder one when we have to come down from this whole thing." That was all the prodding Ed would require. Getting himself stuffed back inside the spacecraft proved to be no easy task—and remember this was Ed White we're talking about—and once Ed got back in his seat closing the hatch wasn't much easier than opening it had been. Still, they did it and at 5:19:21, Jim reported that the cabin had been resealed and that Ed was safely inside. Gemini IV had made history and, lest the world overlook the fact, NASA made sure to let them know that Ed had stayed outside twice as long as the Bolshevik superman Leonov.

After Ed's spectacular feat, nothing that happened sub-sequently on Gemini IV (short of the loss of one or both crew members) would have been—or should have been—characterized as a failure. The other side of that coin was that everything that happened during the mission after Ed got back inside was going to be anticlimactic. Still, there was the four day duration goal that needed to be achieved and Jim and Ed still had over three days of flying time remaining to do it. On a later revolution, they were scheduled to reopen the hatch and dump all of Ed's EVA equipment overboard. Because the hatch locks had been so balky on the EVA, the decision was made to not risk another hatch opening. This meant that all of Ed's gear was going to have to be stowed and that made for a very cramped spacecraft. White, in fact, had to keep his twenty-five foot EVA tether bundled up in his lap for the remainder of the flight.

During the time after the EVA and before retrofire, Jim and Ed breezed through a series of eleven onboard experiments. Because of the excessive fuel consumption during the great booster chase, they also had to endure an extended period during which the crew floated aimlessly in space. As McDivitt recalled in the post-flight debriefing, "As soon as we finished the EVA, we went into free drifting flight," which Jim described as "a complete power down procedure" in which they stayed for the next 2½ days. Said McDivitt, "At this time of the mission I guess we weren't doing much except staying alive. My impression of what we were doing was eating, sleeping and dumping tapes." To which White added, "And looking at the ground as it went by." Apparently, identifying land masses from space to fill the time adrift was not as easy as in geography class where the color-coded maps had printed names on the individual countries. Once, when Ed thought he was look-ing at Tampico, Mexico when in fact what he was really seeing was Sydney, Australia, McDivitt chided his buddy, saying, "You only missed it by half the world."

After Gemini IV had completed its fourth day in space, it was time for the moment of truth. Gemini IV had come equipped with a small onboard computer that was designed for the primary function of assisting the crew in angling the spacecraft for reentry. During the power down earlier in the mission, McDivitt had tried to shut down the computer but couldn't. Then, the ground gave it a go and also failed. So they told McDivitt to disconnect the computer's power source. That had done the trick but when McDivitt now tried to turn it back on for reentry it wouldn't restart. At 97:06:08, McDivitt stated, "I do still need my computer." Unfortunately, Jim had to advise, "I can't think of any way to bring it up." Now, instead of a controlled reentry, McDivitt would have to fly a manual "rolling" Mercury-type reentry. Thankfully, it was a contingency for which McDivitt, a brilliant pilot, was well trained. Once Jim got the spacecraft lined up and the adapter section jettisoned at 97:39:20, the four retrorockets were fired slowing the vehicle and Jim then executed the rolling reentry perfectly. Oscillations from the drogue and the main chutes made life interesting for a few minutes during their descent and they hit the ocean like a hammer but Gemini IV was down and Jim and Ed were safe.

Once they'd landed, Jim asked Ed how he was doing. When White grinned and replied, "Just fine," Jim said jokingly, "I guess we aren't going to die after all." None of the potential medical problems predicted prior to the mission manifested themselves during the crew's post-flight physicals prompting Kraft, never a fan of NASA's medical prophets of doom, to happily observe, "The doctors had no choice but to accept the results." That meant that NASA flight surgeon Dr. Charles Berry and his staff had no reason to throw up any roadblocks to obstruct Kraft and the rest of the NASA brass from pursuing their next goal—an eight day mission.

THE FINAL SCORECARD FOR the Gemini IV mission had been an impressive one. Even though the booster rendezvous attempt had failed, Ed's spectacular success on the EVA—he had stayed out twice as long as Leonov, remember– had rendered that failure a footnote. Further, the crew had stayed up virtually as long as any Russian crew or spacecraft ever had proving that neither the

Soviet's hardware or their cosmonaut training procedures were in any way superior to that of their American counterparts. Even better, on top of all of Gemini IV's successes was NASA's real ace in the hole which was the proven maneuvering capability of the Gemini spacecraft. Although no one in the Kremlin was ever going to confirm it, NASA's flight team was beginning to suspect that neither Vostok or Voskhod had any such capability. Whatever the case, this race to the moon was obviously no longer a one-sided affair. With the success of Geminis 3 and IV, the American people were beginning to think that maybe—just maybe—the Russians weren't as invincible as they had appeared to be ever since the launch of Sputnik eight years ago and that maybe—just maybe—the United States might have a shot at winning the race after all.

# CHAPTER 3

# Eight Days in a Garbage Can

The crew selection criteria which Deke Slayton set forth in his 1994 autobiography "Deke" were unknown to the members of the astronaut corps during his years as Chief of Flight Crew Operations. That's exactly the way Deke wanted it. Guys have a tendency to get complacent when they're comfortable and Deke figured he could count on getting maximum effort from every single astronaut in the office provided that he could keep each of them guessing about where they stood in the grand scheme of things. Still, whatever the criteria were, there was obviously a method to the madness particularly when it came to Deke's uncanny ability to marry up the individual crew members for specific missions. On Gemini 3, John Young's laconic wit and low-key charm proved to be a great fit with the hard-charging intensity of Grissom. As to Gemini IV, McDivitt and White had practically been brothers before ever joining NASA so that one was pretty much a no-brainer. So far so good. But Gemini V was gonna be a real head-scratcher for Slayton. The problem confronting Deke: What poor soul do you cram into a space the size of the passenger's seat of a Volkswagen Beetle next to Gordo Cooper? For eight goddamn days. It was going to be a horribly tough call and, if he didn't make the right one, Deke might just have to have Guenter Wendt and his boys down at the pad weld the hatch door on the pilot's side shut right before launch just to insure that the guy didn't try to bail out of the spacecraft during the mission. Fortunately, Deke came through.

Charles Conrad, Jr. was born on June 2, 1930 in Philadelphia to Charles, Sr. and his strong-willed wife, Frances, who insisted that the boy be called Peter even though that name would not appear on the child's birth certificate. Born to privilege, young Peter attended the venerable Haverford School in the Pennsylvania town of the same name. There, as a fourth grader, he was chosen to play the Virgin Mary in the 1939 Haverford Christmas Tableaux. During the production's sixth and final night, the kid playing Joseph had one too many Christmas cookies, succumbed to the heat of the bright lights and threw up all over the Blessed Virgin. Young Peter then ripped off his puke-soaked costume and, onstage and in his underwear, beat the living snot out of Vomiting Joseph. All while the cream of Haverford society beheld Peter's version of the Christmas miracle and collectively gasped in mortification. Yeah, the kid was a handful. That a boy like Peter would never quite flourish at a place like Haverford should have come as no great surprise to anyone and, after accumulating a still-unbroken record for demerits, he would go on to finish his prep school days at the Darrow School in New Lebanon, New York. From there, Peter headed to Princeton from which he graduated in 1953. Then it was on to the Navy where he would eventually end up at Pax River serving as a test pilot, test pilot instructor and performance engineer.

That's the NASA bio. But no dry-as-the-Sahara résumé could ever do justice to a guy so much larger than life than Pete (he would eventually dump the "r") Conrad. At 5'6" ½—and he never left out the "½"—Conrad was the only astronaut in the first three classes who was actually shorter than Gus Grissom. A poster child for male-pattern baldness with a gap between his two front teeth large enough to accommodate a McDonald's french-fry, Pete was a wisecracking machine who could outjoke—and outcuss—any nightclub comedian who ever came down the pike. The idea of frequenting a tavern and having a drink or eight never troubled him either and if some 6'2" jarhead (God help anyone who wasn't a Navy man) was there running his mouth, Pete just might walk up to him, place a crooked index finger under the bill of his ballcap and then flip it up and over the top of his head. And if the guy did anything other than bend down and silently pick up his cap then the shit was gonna hit the fan. You see, nobody—absolutely nobody—ruled Pete Conrad's roost except Pete Conrad.

Being such a colorful guy, it was only natural that Pete would learn to fly in an unconventional way. For a couple of years during his teens, Pete had been knocking around the Paoli Airfield sweeping the floors and doing odd jobs to earn a few bucks but mostly—and, as of mid–1947, unsuccessfully—trying to find someone willing to teach him how to fly an airplane. Then one evening, the Paoli Field phone rang and rang and with Pete finally yelling an "All right!" he picked up the receiver and ran ear-first into a profane harangue coming from a decidedly feminine voice on the other end of the line. Pete stammered, "Well I'm sorry, Mrs…" only to have that met with "That's *Miss* Lowell, broom boy." Pete somehow gathered himself and ascertained that Miss Lowell's plane, which was serviced by Pete's boss, had konked out several miles away forcing her to make an emergency landing in a cornfield. After grabbing some tools and parts, Pete hopped on his motorcycle and managed to track down the exceptionally pissed-off Miss Lowell. Describing her as attractive "in a Rosie the Riveter kind of way" and finding her in the company of a female companion dressed like a housewife of the era, Pete introduced himself and quickly patched up the plane and then hopped back on his bike for the trip home. After finding that the two ladies had beaten him back to Paoli Field, Pete politely refused Miss Lowell's offer of ten dollars to compensate him for his trouble. When she asked if there was anything else she could do, Pete sheepishly replied, "You could teach me to fly." Taking Pete up on it, Miss Lowell cut Pete loose to solo after his sixth lesson. Once he'd successfully completed the one hour flight, Pete was so excited that he leapt out of the cockpit with the prop still turning. Sighting Miss Lowell seated at a nearby picnic table accompanied by the same woman she was with the night he'd met her, Pete ran up and euphorically planted a kiss right on Miss Lowell's lips. This, in turn, prompted Miss Lowell's companion to leap up and unleash a haymaker at the side of Pete's head which Miss Lowell fortuitously managed to intercept. By now this was a situation absolutely overbrimming with self-evident truths but this being 1947 and all and Pete only being 16 years old and all … well, let's just say it was a couple more years before Pete connected all of the dots concerning Margaret Lowell and then leaned back with a vacant expression and thought "Oh…"

As a Pax River instructor, Pete was a natural choice for inclusion in the first batch of 110 test pilots who were invited to try out for Project Mercury. Pete then made the cut by NASA's Aeromedical Committee down to the 36 who were invited to Albuquerque's Lovelace Clinic for several more days of intensive physical and psychological testing—with resounding emphasis being placed on the intensive part. As bad as the endless x-rays and sampling of bodily fluids were, the real rub for Pete was the psychological testing. One aspect of NASA's head-probing included what was called a Rorschach Test which presumably was named after the chain-smoking monacle-wearing goateed weirdo who'd thought it up. Administration of the "test" such as it was consisted of presenting each prospective astronaut with a piece of white paper containing various shapes of an ink blot. The examiner would then ask the candidate, who had only seconds to respond, what the ink blot was or what it represented. God only knows what the testing was actually intended to reveal but a consensus quickly developed among the candidates that the Rorschach was nothing more than a ruse designed to suss out any hint of non-heterosexuality in the candidate being tested. This, in turn, led every candidate to describe every ink blot regardless of shape as some part of a woman's reproductive anatomy. The situation reached the peak of absurdity when guys that were being shown ink blots that were obviously penis-shaped were still describing them as "Brigitte Bardot" and "Uh, y'know … tits." Then, one day one of the shrinks got the bright idea to test Conrad by handing him a totally blank white sheet of paper. Pete gazed thoughtfully at the paper for a moment, then turned it twice by the corners and shoved it back across the desk at the aspiring Sigmund Freud saying, "Here, you gave it to me upside down." The guy was not even remotely amused and proceeded to kick Pete out of his office.

Finally, by day eleven, Pete had reached his limit. That morning he walked into the base commander's office with that day's dutifully filled enema bag. Leading with, "General, something to remember me by...", Pete tossed the bag of his fecal sample up onto the guy's desk and then turned on his heel and walked straight out the front door of the Lovelace Clinic. Back at Pax River a couple of years later, seeing his old Navy buddy Al Shepard's face plastered across the front page of the New York Times after the flight of Freedom 7, Pete was rapidly coming to the conclusion that the blue ribbon he'd won in the Albuquerque enema bag toss wasn't such a terrific prize after all. Pete had screwed a pooch that he shouldn't have screwed and he knew it. When it came time to give it another go, Pete gritted his teeth and played NASA's game. Perhaps rewarded for his forebearance as much as his perseverance, he was introduced as a member of the New Nine on September 17, 1962. As the pilot on Gemini V, he would become the fourth of them to fly into space.

Then, of course, there was Gordo. Leroy Gordon Cooper, Jr. was born March 6, 1927 in Shawnee, Oklahoma. After being placed on active duty by the Air Force in 1949, he received a B.S. in aeronautical engineering from the Air Force Institute in 1956. After that, it was on to Edwards where he graduated from test pilot school in 1957 and was assigned as an aeronautical engineer and test pilot where he flew experimental fighter aircraft. By the time he was selected as a member of the Mercury Seven, Gordo had logged more than 4,000 hours flying time in jets. Like nearly all of his Mercury brethren, Cooper was an extremely accomplished aviator. Like some of them, he had both a personality and a taste for mischief that could periodically be excessive.

Whether it was attributable to Gordo being a guy living in a constant high-stress environment trying to either blow off steam or trying to show NASA management that he felt underappreciated or whatever it was, sometimes the hot dog from Oklahoma just didn't know when to let up—or shut up. It wasn't that Gordo was the bad seed exactly, just more like a class clown who didn't understand when enough was enough. Before Mercury had ever flown, NASA was (as always) thinking of ways to curry favor with the national media and they settled upon allowing a TV crew onto the Cape to follow one of the Seven around to film "Launch day in the life of an Astronaut." For some incomprehensible reason NASA picked Gordo for the job and the TV crew eagerly followed him around all day even going so far as to meticulously film him while he was wearing his long underwear. Everything was going just peachy until they all got out to the launchpad. There the TV people dutifully set up shop to document the majestic solemnity of the courageous American space hero striding purposefully forth into the jaws of danger for all mankind to behold. Then, as he got close to the gantry elevator, Gordo grabbed onto the doorway and began screaming hysterically "NO, I WON'T GO … I WON'T GO!," while Guenter Wendt (who was in on the gag) gave the desperate appearance of trying to forcibly drag Gordo onto the elevator. The other astronauts and Guenter's pad guys all thought the whole thing was as funny as hell but the NASA brass, the public affairs office and the TV guys were all just absolutely furious. Then came the aforementioned flaps over the naming of Faith 7 and the one with Walt Williams the day before that mission which nearly got him bumped off the flight.

On the other side of the scale, Gordo had two primary things going for him: First, he'd absolutely flown the living daylights out of Faith 7 battling multiple systems failures and sticking the landing on what was by far the longest and perhaps the most difficult flight of the Mercury program. Second, for now at least, he had Slayton's unwavering support despite the fact that Deke was keenly aware that Gordo was considered a "question mark" by NASA management.

Now, in the leadup to Gemini V, there would be yet another completely avoidable conflict with the brass which would result in a direct faceoff between Gordo and Jim Webb, NASA's Chief Administrator. Webb had made it as clear as crystal after the Molly Brown flap prior to Gemini 3 that after that flight there would be no more individual names for spacecraft other than the mission's designation. McDivitt and White got the message and tactfully didn't even raise the issue during the planning stages for Gemini IV despite the fact that McDivitt had wanted to name the spacecraft. Rather than allow the matter to remain settled in accordance with his boss's wishes—and in another remarkable demonstration of just how tone-deaf he could be—Gordo started hammering away at Webb trying to convince him to reverse course and rescind the no-naming policy despite the fact that it had been in effect for just one flight. Webb flatly refused. Unwilling to let the matter drop, Gordo then dangled the carrot that he and Pete just might be amenable to naming the spacecraft "Ladybird" in honor of President Lyndon Johnson's wife. Webb still said no. So, going back to the drawing board, Gordo determined that if he couldn't name the spacecraft, then he wanted to commemorate the mission with a patch, which up to that time had never been done before. Then, he decided that he and Pete should fly from the Cape to Houston to pitch the idea to Webb personally rather than have Webb somehow hear of the proposal secondhand. At dinner that night, Gordo presumptuously took aim at the man who was essentially NASA's CEO, leading with, "Jim, you've taken our spacecraft names away from us, and as you know, none of us particularly like it…Pete and I want to personalize our flight, and we've designed a really neat mission patch." How Webb summoned the self-control not to reply, "Well Gordo, once again you've violated my direct orders and I don't particularly like that. I want to ground the two of you and you can stick your mission patch up your asses" God only knows. Still, Gordo later acknowledged that "Webb about went into hysterics" at the suggestion. Imagine that. The discussion eventually degenerated into an argument so heated that Bob Gilruth and Gordo had to physically separate Webb and Conrad. After everyone cooled down, Gordo eventually began to sway Webb with the bullshit notion that this was all about "team-building" and morale and the camaraderie that wearing the same mission patch would engender amongst the launch and flight control teams. Perhaps viewing it from that perspective or perhaps simply wanting to extract this particular thorn from his asscheek, Webb relented with the caveat that he—Webb—would have final approval concerning the design of the patch. Gordo then responded by submitting the Gemini V mission patch which featured a Conestoga wagon with the slogan "8 Days or Bust" emblazoned above it. Of course, Webb nearly busted an artery when he saw the goddamned slogan and immediately (and correctly) surmised that the media and especially the Russians would declare the mission a "Bust" if Gordo and Pete didn't last the entire eight days. Accordingly, Webb demanded that the slogan be somehow eliminated or at least covered over until the mission had been successfully completed. This time Gordo relented for a change and had little pieces of canvas sewn over the slogan which would not be removed prior to splashdown. Now that this most critical of issues had been laid to rest, NASA could finally get on with such trifling details as trying to figure out exactly which objectives they wanted to accomplish during the mission and how best to achieve them.

Of course, the most important mission objective was—far and away—achieving the goal of having both the Gemini V spacecraft and the crew survive an eight day mission in space. That objective was simple enough to comprehend in theory but the fact was that it was twice as long as any spacecraft, American or Russian, or any astronaut or cosmonaut had ever spent outside the Earth's atmosphere. Although easily stated, it was going to be a monumental challenge for the astronauts, the flight control team and the spacecraft itself and everybody at NASA knew it.

Up to this time, why hadn't the United States been able to put a spacecraft into orbit for longer than four days? In a word—weight. Because of the thrust limitations of the Titan II (as well as those of the Redstone and Atlas before it), there was a finite amount of weight that the rocket, when used as a launch vehicle for a spacecraft, could lift off the ground. Because batteries were heavy and could not regenerate themselves in flight, the McDonnell guys could only stuff and stack enough batteries onboard a Gemini spacecraft to keep it aloft for four days. Because the ultimate goal of the NASA program was to land a man on the moon *and* return him safely to Earth and the fact that the most optimistic of estimates indicated that it was going to take at least eight days to accomplish such a mission, the mathematics of the situation were quite clear. Obviously, NASA or McDonnell or somebody was going to have to develop an onboard power source that was both lighter and which could last longer than the batteries that had been used to power every American spacecraft up to this point. That's why the development of fuel cell technology was so crucial. It had to work or the United States wasn't going to the moon by the end of the decade. Gemini V would be its first use in manned spaceflight.

Then, of course, there was the human element. Having a spacecraft that was capable of traveling to and from the moon would be of little use from a manned spaceflight perspective if the human body could not withstand the rigors of the journey. Unfortunately, there was no way to simulate extended periods of microgravity within the Earth's atmosphere. The only way that NASA could devise for astronauts to experience even brief periods of weightlessness was to place them in the padded fuselage of their KC-135 aircraft (dubbed the "Vomit Comet" by the astronauts for the highly efficient manner in which it induced nausea) and fly them in parabolic arcs which during the drop phase would produce weightless periods of up to forty seconds. For whatever use that was (and some astronauts thought it wasn't much), it certainly could not simulate the effects that continuous microgravity would have on the human body for over a week. Unfortunately, the only way to find out what those effects were was to send the crew of Gemini V up there for that long and then see what happened to them both in flight and after splashdown. It was great that McDivitt and White had survived for four days on the previous flight and had seemed no worse for wear after taking a couple of days to recover. As for staying up there twice that long, Gordo and Pete were simply going to be human laboratory specimens.

As for the remaining objectives of the mission, they could fairly be categorized as secondary goals. The most important of them would be an attempted rendezvous with "a free flying optical and electronic device with a flashing light and transmitting-receiving beacon known as the Rendezvous Evaluation Pod (REP)." It would be released from the adapter module in flight and then tracked using onboard radar which would be the first usage of that technology in space as well. Any information gleaned from this exercise could be of importance to future rendezvous and docking missions later in the program. In addition, the crew was to have an onboard computer which they hoped would function better than the one on Gemini IV. Finally, there would be the usual complement of scientific experiments, the most interesting of which would involve visual acuity and trying to identify, as well as photograph, specific objects on the ground from orbit. The pictures obtained during the photographic experiments would lead to a very interesting post-mission conversation between Gordo and President Johnson.

Gemini V was given a go for launch on August 19, 1965 and Pete and Gordo went through the pre-launch breakfast and suiting ritual. However, after they were loaded into the spacecraft, it didn't take long for problems to arise. First, a glitch cropped up in the topping off of the fuel cells, then a thunderstorm hit the Cape during which a lightning strike caused a burp in the spacecraft's power supply. As Conrad put it, "All power dropped off the space-craft—and the rest of the pad for the matter—while the lightning hit whatever it was, a transformer somewhere in the vicinity of the Cape. I can remember very well turning to Gordo—I think we were at about t-minus ten minutes in the count—to say 'Well, I think that's it for the day!' Because every gauge in the thing went to zero and came back on again. There was no way, in my mind, NASA would ever launch us having a glitch like that go through the system." Pete had called it and Kraft scrubbed the launch as if on cue. The erector stand was brought in and raised and Guenter and his guys went up and pried the crew out. Then, all the propellants had to be drained from the Titan II necessitating a forty eight hour minimum turnaround for the next launch attempt.

The weather at the Cape cleared sufficiently for NASA to once again attempt to get Gemini V off the pad and at precisely 9:00 a.m. on August 21, 1965 the Titan sprang to life. Gordo greeted the liftoff with "We're on our way" followed seconds later with "Been a long time getting back." At 7:17, Capcom relayed that they were in an 85 by 199 mile orbit. While the crew did experience some jerky bouncing of the Titan (called "Pogo" by NASA) during the first stage, Gordo dubbed the booster a "Cadillac" compared to his previous ride on the Atlas. Things went smoothly through the first orbit. However, shortly after deploying the rendezvous pod at 2:13:45, the crew began to notice a serious anomaly in the fuel cells. Why was this critical? As Gordo put it, "Proving that we could fly with a fuel cell was paramount. Unlike batteries, which consume themselves, fuel cells are almost endlessly rechargeable as long as there is a fuel source to provide hydrogen. A fuel cell is operated by the chemical reaction of hydrogen and oxygen and requires that high pressure be maintained in cryogenic (low temperature) storage tanks so that sufficient amounts of fuel can be stored to provide high electrical output." In other words, if a fuel cell died, electrical power to the spacecraft would cease. While a stack of batteries was placed onboard as a backup power supply and for use during reentry, the ship could not stay aloft for any significant period of time with a dead fuel cell. At 2:23:19 Pete called out "That fuel cell O2?" Then seconds later, "How the heck did that get that low?" After starting out with a pressure of 850 PSI, at 2:48:46, Gordo pegged the PSI at 120 and had started to power down the spacecraft. That did not bode well for Gemini V.

In Mission Control, Kraft had ordered the REP maneuver canceled and that "only the most critical onboard systems would stay on-line. Everything else drawing electricity was being turned off." By 3:10:19, Gordo had grasped the severity of the situation copying that Gemini V had to "power down" or the mission was going to have to be aborted. Somewhere at NASA Headquarters, Jim Webb was wiping his brow and thanking the Almighty that he'd made Gordo and Pete sew those little pieces of canvas over that damn "8 Days or Bust" slogan.

Now, Kraft had to make a call. If he didn't bring them down by the fourth orbit, he'd have to either wait a day until the prime Atlantic recovery zones were once again available or be forced to bring them down in a remote location where the recovery forces would be farther away and perhaps even out of communications range. At 5:50:15 Gordo said to Pete, "Suppose they'd have the courage to run us for 8 days like this" to which Pete replied, "Boy, I don't know." Gordo then said wistfully, "I kind of doubt it." A few minutes later, Pete said, "You better not go with me again Gordo; I must be unlucky here." Unlucky for Pete, sure. But poor Gordo. Twice he'd risked his ass being blasted into space and once again he'd found himself in drifting orbital flight with a powered down spacecraft, just as he had on Faith 7.

By 6:03:34, Pete reported that the fuel cell O2 tank pressure had stabilized "right at 60" PSI. Kraft then made the call. Assured that the spacecraft had thirteen hours of battery power remaining, Kraft gave the order to continue the flight to which Gordo replied, "Let's give it a go." Gordo was instructed at 7:48:10 to go to batteries if the fuel cell failed which in turn meant the mission would be aborted after a maximum of one day in orbit. At the handover to Kranz at the end of Kraft's shift, Kranz asked his boss what he wanted him to do. Kraft gave his protégé all the guidance and advice he'd ever need for the rest of his career when he replied, "You're the flight director, it's your shift. Make up your own mind." Kranz would never again need to be reminded that he was now in the big leagues.

When the fuel cell oxygen pressure problem was still in a stable condition at the end of the thirteen hour window, the decision was made to forge ahead with a go/no-go decision to be made at the end of each day. With the REP maneuver canceled, Flight Director John Hodge had devised a maneuver which Mission Control dubbed a "phantom rendezvous" in which the ground essentially gave the crew an aiming point in space where a theoretical Agena target vehicle would be waiting for them. This, the media was told, would simulate Gemini VI's planned rendezvous with an actual target vehicle. Using ground radar to track the spacecraft's path, NASA determined that the crew had performed the theoretical "rendezvous" successfully. That would have to suffice until a later mission when NASA could try it for real.

From that point on, it was going to be a grind for Gemini V. NASA's euphoria from just getting into space, followed by Glenn's first orbit and Ed's spacewalk was now giving way to the harsh realization that the mundane everyday tasks that must be accomplished to survive on the ground must also be attended to in space. That these guys had to be able to efficiently eat, drink, sleep and, yes, go to the bathroom within the confines of the spacecraft were all tasks that had to be performed with constant (and you better believe constant) supervision from NASA medical personnel back in Mission Control. Along with that there was endless monitoring of body temperature, cabin temperature, suit temperature, blood pressure and the amount of exercise (with a bungee cord) being performed inside the spacecraft. It was a grind which Pete recalled in the following way, "The romance ended fairly quickly. We were really confined in an extremely small space. My knees began to bother me. It felt as though my knee sockets had gone dry. I hurt and I didn't want to stay in there. If they told me I had to stay up there longer than the eight days I would have gone bananas. My body ached and my mind was not active enough. I was the rookie and Gordo was the pro. We trained together for a year and there weren't any stories left to exchange. We had some systems failures, and this precluded us from doing some of the tasks we were supposed to do, so all we could do is sit. You can't go to sleep; you just don't get tired. Your body is uncomfortable, you don't do any work and zero G makes you lethargic. We didn't have continuous communications with Earth and there was an eight hour sleep time when the ground wouldn't talk to us. We had thruster failures on the third day and we spent a lot of time in drifting flight. It didn't take long to realize that eight days was going to be an extremely long period of time. Houston had ordered us to shut down due to the thruster failure. Gemini would vent oxygen and hydrogen occasionally. Whenever it vented, it would give the capsule a little motion and it would rotate ... it was very frustrating. Whenever we were over land, which was the one thing that was always fun to look at, the craft would be pointing up at the black sky. I was the loneliest I have ever been ..." So it went. And so much for the glamour of spaceflight.

As Kranz would later state, "We limped through the flight of Gemini V one day at a time." After the fuel cell O2 pressure problem had stabilized, the crew then began to experience problems with the OAMS thrusters used to both maneuver and stabilize the spacecraft in orbit. This, coupled with everything else going on inside the ship, led to the necessity for the long periods of drifting flight described by Conrad. The crew was able to occupy themselves throughout the mission with both visual acuity and photography experiments during which Gordo would maneuver the spacecraft such that both astronauts could attempt to see and/or take pictures of various objects on the Earth's surface. It was interesting that these "experiments" seemed to almost exclusively involve sighting "wakes of carriers," "airbases," "planes in flight" and other objects of a seemingly military nature. At 4:02:35:52, Pete reported that he was "taking some more photographs of Cuba" to which Gordo couldn't resist chiming in with a little Cold War humor, "Just scenic shots." Of course boys, of course.

Kraft lit up a cigar at 119 hours, 6 minutes into the flight in recognition of the fact that Gemini V had just surpassed the Russian endurance record for a single spaceflight. When Houston Capcom suggested to Conrad that he perform a victory roll with the spacecraft to commemorate the occasion, Pete radioed back that he simply couldn't spare the fuel. From that point on, it was really just a matter of surviving through to the eighth day. Essentially, the crew was in a weightless ballet where they would roll, yaw or tumble. Then Gordo would correct the situation (i.e. keep any of those movements from becoming too extreme) by using short bursts from the OAMS thrusters to negate or "damp out" the rates. At 5:23:08:39 when asked if he was getting any exercise, Gordo replied that he was holding "Pete's hand once in a while" and that the two of them were "chewing gum." Then, an hour later, to break the monotony Mission Control actually asked which of them had pooped more often during the flight (at that point, Pete was leading 2 to 1). At 6:04:52:09 Pete reported that Gordo was "unable to come to the phone right now" which was a delicate way of saying "Hey look, Gordo's takin' a crap, okay?" 2 to 2. By that time the various tracking stations had taken to piping up music whenever possible to keep the crew's minds distracted and the thruster degradation had progressed to the point that Mission Control was encouraging the guys to just try to get some sleep until retrofire.

Reentry would be the first "to be guided exclusively by a computerized instrument landing system." Pete called "All four retros fired" at 7:22:28:05. The computer was bringing them in too steep so Gordo took over manually and flattened out their descent. The ship came through blackout at 7:22:49:17 and the drogue was out thirty seconds later. The main chute came out on schedule and Gordo radioed the recovery forces that Gemini V was "on the water" at 7:23:04:16. At that point, the crew had a decision to make as airbags inflated around the spacecraft. They could ride it out and the chopper could hoist the ship up with them inside or they could bail out into a life raft and be harnessed up into the chopper for the ride back to the carrier. "What do you think, Pete?" asked Gordo. "It's gotta be a hundred thirty in here, Gordo. I'm sweating my ass off." As the frogman banged on the hatch, Pete called it by saying, "I can't do another minute in here. Open the son of a bitch." Years later when asked about his recollection of Gemini V, Pete would state succinctly, "My best and shortest description was ... eight days in a garbage can."

Back in Mission Control, while the crew was still bobbing on the water, Kraft was about to light his traditional post-flight cigar when one of the FIDO guys came slinking up to his console with one of those "I just found out my dog died" looks on his face. As it turned out, the reason that the computer had tried to bring Gordo in so steep was because, as Kraft stated it, "They forgot the Earth keeps spinning under the spacecraft after retrofire." To make matters worse, at one hundred miles short there was simply no way that the undershoot could be glossed over at the post-flight press briefing. Kraft carefully eyed up FIDO's messenger boy who at that moment undoubtedly wished he'd never been born, and with a particularly wicked Kraftian look said, "I assume that this won't happen again." Unsurprisingly, it never did. Still, blue collar folks across the country watching "As The World Turns" on their black and white television sets had a good laugh when they found out that NASA's golden boys had theorized at the end of Gemini V that all of a sudden it no longer did.

Back on the carrier, Gordo and Pete finally got to remove the canvas strips covering their "8 Days or Bust" logo. Both had suffered some losses in blood plasma volume but to the relief of NASA's flight surgeons they were physiologically "almost" back to normal within 48 hours. The mission, although trumpeted by both the press and NASA as a glorious success, had unfortunately still not silenced the rumblings about Gordo. While he had undoubtedly performed very well, perhaps even flawlessly, under the extreme duress of the mission—proving once again that when his butt was on the line Gordo could fly as well as Big Al, Wally and the best of the rest of them—all those "incidents" were starting to weigh against him. The flap with Webb over naming Gemini V and then the patch debate, on the heels of the controversy over naming Faith 7 and then scaring the daylights out of Walt Williams.

Now, to top it all off, came an invitation for Gordo and Pete to dine at the White House after the mission. Prior to the dinner, NASA had classified the photographs that the crew had taken onboard Gemini V. Not knowing the origin of that decision, Gordo was furious about it as he'd wanted the photos made public. At the White House dinner, Gordo, rather than playing the role of the humble and just-honored-to-be-here astronaut, decided to complain about the matter directly to his host for the evening who also happened to be the President of the United States. Lyndon Johnson listened with as much patience and deference as his temperament would permit (which wasn't a hell of a lot on his most indulgent day) but when Gordo's whining reached the level of outright impertinence, Johnson finally thundered, "Son, *I* ordered it classified." Recognizing that a West Texas polecat outranks an Oklahoma hot dog—especially when he's President of the United States—Gordo wisely, albeit reluctantly, shut his yap and let the matter drop. Still, the incident was illustrative of the lack of finesse that Gordo continually displayed when dealing with those above him in the chain of command. That penchant for insubordination may have been something he could have overcome had Gordo had the work ethic of Grissom or even "Ten o'clock Wally" Schirra. But on top of all of Gordo's shenanigans, a joke had already begun to percolate throughout the Astronaut Office, then Mission Control and finally NASA Headquarters. The gist of it was that if you really needed to find Gordon Cooper then the last place you wanted to look was inside a NASA mission simulator. As Slayton would later say, Gordo seemed to be "marking time" after Gemini V. Group 2 astronaut Tom Stafford was even more blunt in his assessment of Cooper stating that, "Gordo had a fairly casual attitude toward training, operating on the assumption that he could show up, kick the tires and go ..." Unfortunately for Gordo, even if he was Mercury royalty and an American hero, there was just way too much talent coming up behind him in the Astronaut Office for him to survive the competition any longer. Gemini V would be his last spaceflight. As for his crewmate, well, go figure. Pete Conrad, the guy who'd been busted out at Albuquerque because the NASA shrinks had deemed him "unfit for long duration spaceflight" (well, that and tossing an enema bag full of shit at the base commander) had just flown the longest space mission in human history. His commander may have been on the downhill slide, but Pete Conrad's amazing journey into the heavens was just beginning.

As to the current state of the program, Kraft would recall, "we now held the record for long duration spaceflight, and ... we were well along in qualifying man for the eight day lunar round trip." Still, Kraft wasn't the kind of man who deluded himself.

Plenty of cutting and pasting had had to be done to keep Gemini V aloft for eight days and he was well aware of that fact. Kraft continued, "We still had rendezvous and docking missions ahead, and a fourteen day flight that now had me plenty worried." Then he confided to his deputy Sig Sjoberg, "We're making it look too easy. I hope we don't end up paying a price someday for leaving a false impression." Despite the significant advancements of the Gemini program to this point, a man with Kraft's experience in flight test was not going to allow himself to indulge in anything but optimism tempered with the utmost caution—especially when he knew that he was confronted by an adversary which had already proven itself time and again to be a clever and extremely resourceful opponent.

# CHAPTER 4

# 76

Looking at the Gemini program in 1965 from the outside in, one would have thought that achieving rendezvous had become an obsession with NASA: rendezvous with the spent booster on Gemini IV, followed by rendezvous with the suitcase pod on Gemini V then phantom rendezvous with a point in space on that mission. But rendezvous wasn't truly going to be rendezvous in the eyes of the world until an American spacecraft went into orbit and located another powered vehicle in flight, closed in on it and flew in formation with it—and NASA knew it. Further, the NASA brass had determined that the best way to achieve that goal in the short term was to send up an unmanned "target vehicle" into orbit and then launch a manned Gemini spacecraft to go up and chase it down. That unmanned target vehicle would come to be known as "the Agena."

The Agena target vehicle was actually a two stage vehicle which in NASA parlance was called the Atlas-Agena D. The first stage of the system was quite similar to the old Mercury veteran which was known as the Atlas Standard Launch Vehicle (SLV). Standing 77 feet high and at 10 feet in diameter, the rocket had 320,000 pounds of booster capability, 57,000 pounds of thrust in a single sustainer engine plus two smaller vernier engines for trajectory and final velocity control. Stage 2, the actual Agena, was 27 feet seven inches long and 5 feet in diameter with a self-contained dual propulsion system which was to be used for maneuvering in flight by the crew, Mission Control or both. Although there would turn out to be no need for it on Gemini VI, the Agena was fitted with a docking collar or "adapter" into which the astronaut piloting the Gemini spacecraft would guide the nose end of the vehicle during docking maneuvers. Once docked, both the crew and the flight control team could access a plethora of the Agena's capabilities, the most important of which was the ability to ignite the Agena's engine to facilitate maneuvering the two docked vehicles in space. The Agena was also outfitted with copper "fingers" on the docking cone to conduct static electricity generated by first contact with the spacecraft to a ground inside the Agena and dissipate it at a controlled rate.

Of course, the primary task at hand for Gemini VI was not to physically link up with the Agena, but rather to first demonstrate that a spacecraft could achieve orbital insertion and then just go and find the thing. At this stage of the game, that primary mission objective—rendezvous with another orbiting vehicle—was more than daunting enough of a challenge. If, and only if, the rendezvous maneuvers were successfully completed without excessive fuel consumption would the command be given to go ahead and move in and attempt to physically join up or dock with the Agena. Rendezvous, if it could be achieved, would be a groundbreaking maneuver. The Soviets, with all of their impressive achievements and spaceflight "firsts," had never dared to even attempt a rendezvous in space.

In the context of the big picture, the concept of rendezvous seemed simple enough to comprehend. But the real questions were: (a) why was it so difficult to translate from theory to application?, and (b) why was doing it so absolutely crucial to the overall success of the Gemini program? Taking the second question first, the short answer was mode. Once NASA had committed itself to employing LOR as the chosen method for landing a man on the moon, there could be no turning back if there was to be any hope of achieving John Kennedy's goal of doing it by the end of the decade. LOR had been chosen because it was not going to be possible to take a single ship out to the moon and down to the lunar surface with enough fuel to blast back off it again and return to

Earth without making the vehicle so large that it would be virtually impossible to land on the moon in the first place. That, in turn, necessitated the two spacecraft mode with the smaller lightweight LM. Because of the constraints on the amount of fuel and weight that the ascent stage of the LM could boost back into lunar orbit after the landing, there had to be a second ship—the CSM—waiting in orbit for the crew ascending from the lunar surface in the LM. The LM crew would then physically dock their ship with the CSM and climb through a tunnel connecting the vehicles and the entire crew would return to Earth in the CSM after discarding what remained of the LM while still in lunar orbit. The ever-loving point as far as rendezvous was concerned is that the entire LOR plan simply would not work if the astronauts ascending off the lunar surface in the LM could not locate the CSM as it circled the moon above them. As a result, the bottom line was that an inability to rendezvous meant no LOR and no LOR meant not achieving Kennedy's goal and perhaps never landing on the moon at all.

As to rendezvous theory, why was something so seemingly elementary as finding a way for one object to meet up with another object in orbit turning out to be such a monumental pain in the neck? There were a couple of reasons. The first is that space is big. Even in today's age of global satellite technology, it was still possible in 2014 for Malaysian Airlines Flight 370 to be lost without a trace while in flight. Using that tragedy as a point of reference, consider trying to find an object as small as an Agena in the vastness of space with the extremely limited computer and radar capabilities of the mid-1960s. The second reason was the counterintuitive nature of the task itself. Under normal airplane flight conditions, a pilot tasked with catching up with an aircraft ahead of him will instinctively seek to solve the problem by taking the airplane up to a higher altitude where the air is thinner and then accelerating the vehicle. In fact, that is exactly what Jim McDivitt had attempted to do during the spent booster rendezvous attempt on Gemini IV, only to find himself—without fully grasping why—with the booster gradually drifting farther and farther away. The flaw in that line of thought is that, in the airplane chase scenario, the vehicles aren't far enough off the ground for the curvature of the Earth to have a significant impact on their flight paths. But at one hundred and twenty miles up, it was a whole new ballgame. Now here's the tricky part. A spacecraft orbiting the Earth at 17,500 mph and 50 miles up is moving faster relative to the Earth's surface than an exact duplicate of that spacecraft orbiting at the same speed but 100 miles up. That's because the higher up the spacecraft goes, the more distance the vehicle has to cover to complete one orbit of the planet. Accordingly, trying to catch up with a spacecraft in a lower orbit—or even one in the same orbital plane—was virtually impossible given the fuel constraints necessitated by the size of the Gemini spacecraft.

How then was the task to be accomplished? Eventually, the orbital mechanics experts settled upon a theory. In order to test it, the target vehicle (the Agena) would be blasted into orbit. Then the chasing vehicle (the Gemini spacecraft) would be launched into a *lower* orbit, then by using the OAMS maneuvering capability of the Gemini initially demonstrated by Gus aboard Molly Brown, the pilot would then sequentially—using a series of precisely calculated step-by-step maneuvers—first raise the orbit of the spacecraft placing it in the same orbital plane as the target vehicle, then briefly accelerate to catch up to it and finally perform a braking maneuver to keep from sailing on by. The challenge at that point then shifted to holding contact with the target (called "station-keeping" by NASA) until completion of the maneuver. Although in retrospect it all sounds quite logical, figuring it out at the time turned out to be an extremely arduous task for the brightest bunch of eggheaded MIT types that NASA could assemble and, even then, that was only the theoretical part. Some poor bastard still had to climb inside the can, get blasted off Pad 19 by the Titan into orbit and then somehow manage to pull it all off. Ever since the Meniere's had grounded Shepard and reshuffled the Gemini flight rotation, Deke knew exactly who that poor bastard just had to be.

Walter Marty "Wally" Schirra Jr. was born on March 12, 1923 in Hackensack, New Jersey. His father was an Army flying instructor who flew in combat over France in World War I and survived getting shot down three times in the process. Upon returning home to New Jersey, Wally Sr. and his wife Florence settled in Oradell in the northern part of the state. Once there, the young couple took up barnstorming the countryside in a Curtiss Jenny biplane with Wally Sr. handling the controls while Florence displayed her talents as a wingwalker (and, yes, you read that right) giving it up only when Wally, Jr. was, in her words, "in the hangar." Later in life when Wally would regale people with stories of his adventures—which he did quite often—he wasn't overstating the point when he said that he was literally flying before he was born. Young Wally earned his commission from Annapolis in 1945. From there, he would fly ninety combat missions in the Korean War during which he shot down two Russian-built MIG fighters. By 1958, Wally had settled in at Pax River where he graduated in the fall of that year. Just a few months later, he would be called to test for the NASA program and was accepted as one of the Mercury astronauts in April, 1959. On October 3, 1962, Wally piloted Sigma 7 through a beautiful six orbit mission during which he masterfully conserved fuel, accomplished every major mission objective and landed within sight of the recovery carrier due to the precision of his reentry.

It was during Mercury that Schirra's gregarious nature began to truly manifest itself and become notorious throughout NASA. If Shepard had become the King of the Cape then Wally was unquestionably the lord of the pranksters. The sometimes elaborate jokes (or "gotchas" in Wallyese) would become the stuff of legend. Sabotaging Shepard's Corvette so Al would lose a drag race to Wally's best friend Grissom. Then there was the time when he left a five gallon jug full of yellowish liquid marked "urine sample" on program nurse Dee O'Hara's desk during training for Sigma 7. The showstopper was Big Al's sixth anniversary at NASA party when Wally swapped out the planned video tribute to Shepard with a film which Wally had put together himself. First it showed

Mercury astrochimp Ham getting a medical exam followed by Shepard with a thermometer in his mouth. Next, there was footage of Ham making screechy chimp noises while banging away at the Mercury capsule flight controls followed by Shepard sitting stoically in the cockpit—all to drive home the point that, for all his fame and stature, Al hadn't really done anything on Freedom 7 that the chimp flights hadn't previously accomplished. Before it was over, Wally had put in everything but split-screen footage of Al and the monkey getting side-by-side rectal exams and he'd have put that in too except that there were some things that even NASA wouldn't film for posterity.

His propensity for mischief notwithstanding, don't get the idea that Wally was a frivolous person. He'd known damn good and well since his days flying over Korea that his chosen profession would occasionally bring him face to face with death. That being the case, Wally thought, a guy might as well laugh in death's face along the way to lighten the journey. In Deke's words, Gemini VI was going to be a "very complicated" flight. It was not a job for a court jester and it was a tribute to Wally's attention to detail that Deke had never seriously considered any other astronaut in the program to command the first rendezvous mission. In addition to his well-deserved reputation for precision flying, Wally was also a strictly no-nonsense commander. The skipper of some other Gemini flight could be tasked with cranking the handle on some crazy sea urchin egg experiment but Wally wouldn't stand for any of that kind of shit mucking up *his* flight plan. Wally never took his eye off the big picture—or his place in it—and he wanted streamlined and well-defined big picture objectives, like rendezvous, placed front and center. Fortunately for everyone involved in the mission, Wally would get that—and only that—on Gemini VI.

Deke's choice to fly second seat to Wally on VI was Thomas P. "Tom" Stafford. Born in Weatherford, Oklahoma on September 17, 1930 to Thomas S., the town dentist, and Mary Ellen, Tom grew up on the prairie during the Great Depression. Like many of his colleagues in the Gemini program, he developed an interest in aviation during childhood and built models of aircraft such as Spitfires and the DC-3. An accomplished student with an aptitude for science and engineering, Tom declined a full Navy ROTC scholarship to Oklahoma University (as well as a chance to try out for Bud Wilkinson's football team) for the opportunity to attend the U.S. Naval Academy where he graduated with the Class of 1952. As there was not yet an Air Force Academy and as he wished to fly an F-86E Sabre, Stafford took advantage of an opportunity to join the Air Force straight out of Annapolis where he was commissioned a second lieutenant on June 3, 1952. From there, he would eventually wind up as a test pilot instructor at Edwards. In April, 1962, upon finding out that the NASA height limit had been raised to six feet, Stafford applied for NASA's second group of astronauts and was informed by Slayton that he'd been selected to join the group on September 14, 1962.

Initially slotted to accompany Big Al on Gemini 3, Stafford got bumped onto the backup crew with Wally due to Shepard's Meniere's ordeal and a combination of Grissom's desire to fly with John Young and Deke's reluctance to break up crews once training for a mission had begun. It was a good pairing. In a world populated by Conrads, Shepards and Schirras, Stafford was about as colorful—at least publicly—as your local mortician and that meshed well with Wally who didn't exactly have a regressive personality in any environment. Like a loudmouthed husband coupled with a deferential wife (or vice-versa), conflicts were far less likely to arise when crewmates weren't climbing over the top of one another to get close to anyone who walked into the room with a TV camera and/or a microphone. As to his private life, yeah, there were some whisperings that Tom (like his first Gemini commander) was on a first name basis with more than his share of bartenders both in Houston and at the Cape and that perhaps he may have even shared the occasional intimate moment with women who were not named Mrs. Stafford. Whatever the truth of the matter was, Slayton, adhering to his long-standing policy, didn't object if a guy did a Tijuana hooker in a bathtub full of Jose' Cuervo as long as it didn't affect the guy's job performance *and* he kept it out of the newspapers. For his part, Stafford kept whatever he was doing after hours low key and did his job superbly and, as far as Deke was concerned, that was all that mattered.

The Agena was fueled and ready on Pad 14, a mile to the south, when Wally and Tom were awakened by Shepard on October 25, 1965. In an almost heartwarming sign of the times that would be unthinkable at today's NASA, Stafford recalled that Wally fired up a Marlboro on the way to Pad 16 for their suiting up procedure. The duo were already strapped down inside the Gemini VI cockpit when, at 10 o'clock a.m., General Dynamics launch chief Thomas J. O'Malley pushed the button to ignite the Agena. The flight plan called for the vehicle to complete one full orbit at which time Wally and Tom would be launched aboard Gemini VI with the task of going up and chasing it down. Unfortunately, it didn't take long for the folks assigned with tracking the Agena from the ground to conclude that something had gone horribly wrong with the vehicle. Ground telemetry showed that after the Agena separated from the Atlas booster, it had begun to wobble. When the Agena's main engine subsequently fired, the rocket exploded into five large pieces. Kraft instantly scrubbed Gemini VI's launch, precipitating a ride for the crew back down the gantry elevator which Schirra later said felt like being a kid who got cold feet on the high dive and then had to skulk back down the ladder to a chorus of catcalls from all the other people at the swim club.

What would happen next was not altogether clear at that moment. Undoubtedly, there would have to be an immediate investigation by the Air Force into the Agena failure so that meant that Gemini VI as originally conceived would not be going up anytime soon. With mission commander Frank Borman and pilot Jim Lovell set to fly a fourteen day mission on Gemini VII, which was scheduled as a simple long duration flight similar to Gemini V, it could conceivably be flown ahead of VI. That meant that the program could keep moving forward as scheduled assuming that the Agena problem could be isolated and corrected quickly enough so that Gemini VI could be rescheduled after VII's flight in a timely way. Then, in one of those "a-ha" moments, McDonnell

Aircraft executive Walter Burke and his deputy John Yardley hit upon an idea. Why not send up Gemini VII for use as the target vehicle for Gemini VI? Yes, such a mission would take any potential docking out of the equation but after all the real goal for now was to prove that rendezvous was possible. The proposed plan was not enthusiastically embraced at NASA Headquarters in D.C. so Burke and Yardley took the matter up with Bob Gilruth and George Low in Houston and found those two to be far more receptive to the idea. Still, if it was going to happen, Chris Kraft was going to have to make it happen. After forming a task force and putting Sig Sjoberg on point, Kraft concluded that the joint mission—to be dubbed 7/6—was possible and quickly brought the Gemini Program Office, Gilruth, Slayton and, in just a few days time, the Washington brass on board.

Of course, there were unprecedented logistical issues that would have to be resolved prior to such a bold undertaking. The first problem was that Pad 19 was the only Titan launchpad which NASA had that was configured for Gemini operations. That meant that both spacecraft had to be launched sequentially from the same pad. The problem with that is that rocket launches tend to wreak havoc on launchpads—which is why the individual missions were spaced several weeks apart. Now, NASA would have to repair that damage in a matter of days in order to make the 7/6 plan work. Also, the launch turnaround problem essentially dictated that VII would have to go up first and serve as the target vehicle for VI. As VI was scheduled to be a relatively short flight and the spacecraft was only equipped with batteries for onboard power—no fuel cells—there was no guarantee that the pad crew could make the turnaround and get VII up before VI ran out of power and had to come down. With Gemini VII having the onboard power capability to stay up for fourteen days, at least there was a shot to send VI up after it assuming all went well with the launch complex's refurbishment after the launch of VII. This, of course, dovetailed nicely with the fact that Wally and Tom had trained to rendezvous with a target vehicle whereas the VII crew of Borman and Jim Lovell had not and were much better suited to serve as the target for VI than vice-versa. Then there was the issue of Gemini VII's weight. Because it carried consumables for a fourteen day flight, the Gemini VII spacecraft was 250 pounds heavier than the Gemini VI capsule. That meant that the launch team couldn't simply go out to Pad 19—where GT-VI still stood in launch configuration—and pluck the Gemini VI spacecraft off the top of the stack and then bolt the VII capsule down to take its place. The Titan built for Gemini VI just didn't have enough thrust to get the VII spacecraft into orbit. So that meant that the only possible way to pull the mission off was to disassemble the entire Gemini VI launch vehicle, stow it someplace nearby at the Cape, haul out the Gemini VII launch vehicle, erect and launch it, then bring the Gemini VI launch vehicle back out to Pad 19 and hopefully get Gemini VI assembled and launched while Gemini VII still had at least a couple of days worth of power left before it had to be brought back down. And, as if that were not enough, Kraft and his flight control team also had to figure out how to talk to two orbiting spacecraft up at the same time using a tracking and communications network that wasn't designed for such a task.

Given all the complexity that this newly configured mission entailed, amazingly there were suggestions to add even more items to the flight plan. The first proposal called for Lovell and Stafford to perform a simultaneous EVA that would culminate in Stafford ending up with Borman inside Gemini VII and Lovell inside VI with Schirra. While the VI crew appeared to be bullish on the idea, Borman—perhaps recognizing that this was as harebrained a scheme as any Soviet stunt Khrushchev had ever dreamed up—said there was no way in hell he was going to open Gemini VII's hatch during the flight for any reason. Another idea nixed by Borman was to have a docking mechanism attached to the blunt end of the Gemini VII spacecraft into which Wally would insert the nose end of Gemini VI. Frank didn't want anything—particularly not Gemini VI—in that kind of proximity to any part of his ship—particularly not the heat shield. Borman was adamant. Rendezvous and long duration were enough mission objectives for

Gemini VII, thank you very much. Quite an intense fellow, this Gemini VII commander.

Frank Frederick Borman II was born on March 14, 1928 in Gary, Indiana, the only child of Edwin and Marjorie Borman. Because Frank was a sickly child, the family relocated to Tucson where his health improved dramatically in the cleaner air and more moderate climate. Small and feisty, he was nevertheless a disciplined student who excelled in football at Tucson High School where he was given the rather ungenerous nickname "Squarehead" by his fellow students. Like Stafford and so many of his fellow astronauts from that time, he fell into his fascination with flying and began building model airplanes after an early childhood ride in one of the barnstorming biplanes of the era. Like Pete Conrad, he took flying lessons from a woman using money he'd scraped together entirely on his own. Like fellow Group 2 astronaut Neil Armstrong, he had learned to fly an airplane before he was even old enough to obtain a license to drive a car.

A revealing incident occurred when young Frank, still a teenager, was flying solo returning to Tucson's Gilpin Airport when an unexpected thunderstorm swept into the area. In spite of the turbulence that was vigorously kicking his backside, Frank got the plane down in one piece. It was, Frank said, a "satisfying" experience but one that fell "short of pride because landing that Taylorcraft safely had been something *expected of me*..." In Frank's young mind, you see, it was his duty to land that plane and one was not allowed the extravagance of personal pride simply for doing one's duty. With that kind of moral fiber at that age, it was hardly surprising that Frank would wind up being accepted into the West Point Class of 1950. Once there, he experienced a calling so immersive that he broke up with the young woman (Susan Bugbee) that he would eventually marry explaining that West Point demanded "everything" of him and had completely altered his life's trajectory. The youngster's innate sense of duty would be keenly refined at West Point, and, from that point on, the central focus of Frank Borman's life would always be "The Mission." After graduating eighth in his class, Frank spent the next decade excelling in various assignments before heading to test pilot school at Edwards in 1960. After graduating as the top student in his class, Frank remained at Edwards and was an instructor at the newly minted Aerospace Research Pilot School when he tossed his cap into NASA's ring and was selected as a Group 2 astronaut on September 17, 1962.

In the early astronaut corps, as in most walks of life, there were hard-edged men who tried to force on a congenial face simply because they wanted to be liked by their colleagues and/or be perceived by them to be a nice guy. Curiously, one got the feeling that the exact opposite was true of Frank Borman. It was almost as if he thought that showing kindness or appearing to be too agreeable might be perceived as weakness by the others. So he kept his edge sharp even if it meant that he was never going to win any popularity contests. Add to that that he may as well have had "Nothing is more important than the mission" tattooed on his forehead and it was plainly evident that getting along with his astronaut colleagues—except for fellow West Pointer and kindred spirit Ed White and his friend Jim Lovell—really didn't matter much to him. Frank Borman was at NASA to fulfill a purpose, one that would make his family, NASA, the Army and his country proud. If, in the conduct of doing that, he didn't get invited to go out drinking and skirt-chasing by some of the others, then screw 'em—Frank didn't care about any of that juvenile crap anyway.

Selected to fly second seat to Borman on Gemini VII was James Arthur "Jim" Lovell. Born March 25, 1928 in Cleveland, he was raised in Wisconsin. His father, a coal furnace salesman, died when Jim was twelve years old and his mother then worked as a legal secretary while providing as best she could for her only child. In something of a departure from the astronaut norm, young Jim developed a fascination not with aviation but rather with the mechanics of rocket engines. He proved just how fascinated when he almost blew himself up as a teen while launching a self-built gunpowder fueled rocket that exploded near him. Hoping to forge a career as a rocket engineer and knowing that his mom couldn't afford college, Jim looked to the military. Eventually, he was accepted at Annapolis where he graduated with a B.S. in 1952 and where his senior thesis was devoted to the study of liquid rocket fuels. After following up flight school with six years as a naval aviator and flight instructor, Lovell obtained admittance to the Pax River fraternity where he was a classmate of Schirra and Pete Conrad who had jokingly nicknamed him "Shaky." Then, it was on to Albuquerque where he endured the medical indignities foisted upon the Project Mercury candidates after which he was ordered to a meeting at Wright-Patterson. Led to believe he'd been selected as one of the Mercury astronauts, Jim was crushed when the brass informed him that an anomaly in his liver had been discovered back at the New Mexico chamber of horrors disqualifying him and moving Gus Grissom up to the seventh and final slot. Undeterred, Lovell reapplied and was accepted by NASA as part of the New Nine in September, 1962.

Throughout the years since, Lovell has sometimes been described as "laid-back" and "easygoing" but that doesn't seem entirely accurate given what the man has accomplished and the heights to which he has risen. "Engaging" might be a more apt description. Whatever it was, Lovell was infinitely more approachable than, say, a guy like Shepard who could be a real son-of-a-bitch even during those rare moments when he was actually in a good mood. Perhaps that was why Slayton paired him with the ultra-driven Borman to begin with. Gemini VII was going to push these guys to the limit in some very unglamorous ways and everyone at NASA knew it. That's why no Mercury veteran wanted any part of it. And, as Lovell would later wryly muse, "Two weeks with Frank Borman anyplace was a challenge." But two weeks side-by-side with him in a space the size of the inside of a telephone booth? It was going to be an asskicker but that's precisely what Jim Lovell had signed up for.

In a departure from NASA's norm of early morning launches, the candle under Gemini VII was lit at 2:30 p.m. on December 4, 1965. The deviation was necessitated by the desire to place Gemini VII in the best possible position in orbit for Gemini VI to catch up with it in a fuel–efficient way after VI's launch scheduled for nine days hence. Once the pad cooled down, it would become the duty of launch operations to take all the necessary steps to assure that the launch of Gemini VI took place within that nine day window. In the meantime, it became the duty of Frank Borman and Jim Lovell to boldly go where Gordo Cooper and Pete Conrad had already gone before. In later years, both Borman and Lovell would refer to themselves in the context of their Gemini VII flight as "guinea pigs." As unflattering as the description sounds, it was appropriate. Primarily, what Frank and Jim had to demonstrate was that a human organism could survive for two weeks in the weightless environment of space. For a generation that has borne witness to astronauts living for months on end in the International Space Station, this may seem a bit archaic. But in the mid-1960s, no one had ever done it before and the only way to find out if it was possible was to send two astronauts up there for that long and then wait and see if they came back alive. Within the parameters of that basic goal was an extremely prolonged exercise in the mundane. First, from a medical standpoint, there were scores of body temperature and blood pressure readings throughout the entire mission which served as a series of data points to be plotted by the flight surgeon's team. In addition to the generation of raw medical data, Frank and Jim had to meticulously monitor and report their intake of both food and water. On top of that, there was the issue of sleeping. Initially, NASA had wanted one astronaut to remain awake at all times during a mission. The problem with that was that when one crewman tried to sleep the activities of the other crewman in combination with the radio chatter from the ground kept that guy awake. Also, there was the whole going-to-the-bathroom thing. So it went. Stay alive and send back data. For nine days. Until Wally and Tom arrived for the rendezvous.

The beginning of Borman and Lovell's travails happened a couple of days into the mission when a urine sample bag burst open and, because of the weightless environment, the crew was never able to truly clean the discharge up. His buddy Conrad might have been able to boast about having spent eight days in a garbage can but now Lovell could one-up him by pointing out that at least Pete hadn't had to spend two weeks in a men's room.

At the bus station. Then, there was the problem with their suits. Both men wanted to remove their heavy flight suits once they were in orbit and fly the mission, at least up until the rendezvous, in the long underwear-type garments they were wearing underneath. When the request was kicked upstairs, the brass kicked it back down with a resounding "No!" In case of an inflight emergency, they wanted both astronauts in pressure suits. Finally, after both their body temperatures began rising, the brass relented and allowed Lovell—but only Lovell—to remove his suit 45 hours into the flight. Borman continued on in the bulky pressure suit which limited his mobility and in which Chris Kraft would point out, "When something itches, scratching is a real chore. After a few days in the same underwear, I had to assume that scratching was on Borman's mind a lot." Indeed. Borman, being Borman, stuck it out for over four more *days* before the guys upstairs finally relented and let both men go pressure-suitless except for rendezvous and reentry. After circularizing their orbit on day five, the only real excitement was seeing who would break first in the battle of the bowel movements. Annapolis vs. West Point. Eyeball to eyeball. Finally, on day nine, Borman blinked. "Jim, I think this is it" said Borman. In typical Lovell fashion, Jim replied, "Aw Frank, couldn't you just wait five more days?"

The good news down at the Cape after VII's launch was that the damage it had inflicted on Pad 19 was minimal. Accordingly, pad reconfiguration for Gemini VI's scheduled launch began almost immediately and, amazingly, the crew got the Titan booster upright and mated the Gemini VI spacecraft atop it—in *one day*. After a week of checkout procedures, NASA was ready and the go was given to launch Gemini VI on December 12, 1965.

Early in the morning on December 12th, Wally and Tom again went through the Pad 16 ritual (no cigarette this time for Wally, Tom observed) and were soon once again strapped down inside Gemini VI sitting on top of the Titan as the countdown to launch proceeded. With no Agena launch to worry about and their rendezvous target aloft and flying beautifully, both astronauts had every reason to believe that today was Gemini VI's day. Six seconds after

9:54 a.m. at the Cape, the launch command was given. Gemini VI's computer light came on and the mission clock started forward. Then … nothing. The Titan just sat there. Like a goddamn totem pole. Five seconds went by. Then ten. It was clear by then that Wally wasn't going to punch out. If he was going to, he'd have done it already. Now, if things went south, Wally and Tom would be engulfed in what Kranz and his boys called the BRFC (Big Red Fucking Cloud). Every asshole in Mission Control was puckered as Wally's voice came crackling through the intercom, "We're just sitting here breathing…" If the Titan blew now—on national television—everyone in the room knew this was either going to be a public relations disaster of the highest order or a game-changer that could end the program entirely. A PR disaster if Tom's boots came down on a highway in Kissimmee and Wally's helmet landed in a swimming pool in Tallahassee. A program-ender if a freckle-faced Cub Scout named Timmy fished the helmet out of the pool and Wally's fucking head was still inside.

If anyone at NASA had ever wondered if Wally really had a pair, their doubts were erased in those first moments after the Titan shutdown. The safer play would have been to reach down between his legs, pull the "D"-ring under his seat and blast both he and Tom clear of the launch vehicle by engaging the spacecraft's ejection seats. But that course of action had drawbacks and Wally knew it. First, just because it was "safer" than potentially getting vaporized in a Titan explosion didn't mean it was safe. Both astronauts would be subjected to horrendous G-forces while getting thrown clear of the launchpad and there wasn't any ironclad guarantee that their chute would open if they cleared the fireball. Second, engaging the ejection seats would have completely wrecked the Gemini VI spacecraft and killed the mission. In weighing the variables, Wally employed what he called "butt-logic" stating, "… I knew in milliseconds that something had gone wrong, that we had not lifted off. Having had the experience of lifting off in Mercury, I knew the difference. I had my butt working for me." Knowing that a guy should never ignore his butt, Wally kept his hands off the "D"-ring. It was one of the gutsiest decisions in the history of American spaceflight—and it saved the 76 mission.

It was later determined that two separate problems had caused the engine shutdown. First, an electrical plug had disconnected from the Titan too soon causing an immediate engine shutdown. Second, a plastic dust cover was discovered in an engine inlet which should have been removed by the pad crew prior to the launch. The amazing thing is that if the second anomaly had occurred on its own then the engine shutdown would not have occurred until two seconds after launch which would have caused the Titan (which would have not yet built up the requisite thrust to keep rising) to come back down onto the pad. As such an event would have undoubtedly caused the rocket to explode, engagement of the ejection seats would have been mandatory—assuming Wally reacted quickly enough to grab the "D"-ring. Some days somebody's just looking out for you. As for Stafford, he didn't make any bones about it. The double malfunction, he said, "really saved our lives."

While they both could have had catastrophic consequences, fortunately neither the plug problem or the dust cover screw-up caused any appreciable damage to the Titan and were easily corrected. With Gemini VII's two week window rapidly closing, that was the kind of news NASA needed to hear. Needless to say, Wally and Tom—having now endured two scrubs of the Gemini VI launch—were both chomping at the bit. The third launch attempt was scheduled for December 15th. This time all finally went as planned. Capcom confirmed liftoff at 1:37 p.m. and five seconds later Wally confirmed that the mission clock had started and that this time "It's a real one." At 6:17 Wally confirmed that Gemini VI was in orbit. After making an orbit to settle in, Schirra got to work. At 1:34:27, Wally called down that the 23 second height adjustment burn had been completed. The process of making the first rendezvous between two vehicles in space had begun. 45 minutes later, the so-called "catch-up" maneuver was achieved, then the 40 second "plane change" burn was completed at 2:42:47.

At 3:28:25, the first radio contact between two manned American spacecraft was achieved when Schirra copied Borman's transmission from three seconds earlier. Wally confirmed that VI was still below VII but added, "Hang on, we'll be up there shortly." After a co-elliptical burn six minutes later, Wally was still showing 60% OAMS fuel remaining which meant, in short, that he was absolutely flying the daylights out of Gemini VI. Just at four hours up, Wally called that he was 154 miles out. A little over an hour later, Schirra acquired a lighted target which he thought might be a star. Stafford excitedly corrected him, blurting out "That's VII, Wally!" At 5:12:39 Schirra called out target confirmed and sixteen minutes later Tom prodded Wally, "Go get him." At 5:50:31, Stafford instructed Schirra to "Stand by to brake."

Four minutes later, at 5:54:29 Lovell called out that Gemini VI was within 120 feet of Gemini VII to which Wally joyfully responded, "Hello there!" The first rendezvous between two manned spacecraft in the history of human spaceflight had been achieved. Two minutes later, Wally famously called "We're all sitting up here playing bridge together," and minutes later, "In formation with VII and everything is GO here." Now came the next hurdle which was determining if VI could hold station with VII—especially during a night pass. Wally reported no trouble as VII's cabin lights kept him apprised of its location. At one point, VI even got close enough (6 to 8 inches away by Wally's estimate) for the crew to see that Borman hadn't shaved since VII's liftoff. Then, prior to the conclusion of their three orbit ballet, it was time for the King of the Gotchas to strut his stuff. Back during training, Schirra and Stafford had decided to have a little fun at Frank Borman's expense. While flying in close formation, they radioed Lovell that NASA's flight surgeon was concerned about the effects that the long duration flight was having on the VII crew's visual acuity. Then, Stafford asked them to look out at VI, take a photograph and then describe what they saw. As West Pointer-for-life Borman looked out his window on VII, the two Annapolis graduates on VI held up a blue and gold sign which read: BEAT ARMY. Characteristically, Borman wasn't particularly amused.

Following the Annapolis pep rally, Wally and Tom thrusted back ten miles and then called it a night. At 22:33:05 after a series of Mission Control-ordered radar lock-ons, Wally showed his teeth a bit, stating that tracking VII "proves we're able to rendezvous and we've done that." As in, "Cut the crap, Houston, I need to get my cockpit squared away before retrofire." After accepting a bet from Borman over who would land closest to the carrier during splashdown, one might have thought Wally would be ready to bring down the curtain on Gemini VI but the old master still had one late-December gotcha up his sleeve. At 23:57:30, Schirra called to VII, "We have an object, looks like a satellite going from North to South, probably in a polar orbit. He's in a very low trajectory travelling from North to South and has a very high climbing ratio." UFOs had been all the rage in the flying saucer-crazed 1950s. Could Schirra be seeing a UFO now? Just as everyone in Mission Control sat up and leaned forward toward their consoles for Wally's next call, he began tooting out the notes to "Jingle Bells" on a four-hole harmonica while Stafford shook a tiny strand of bells in the background. A vintage Schirra moment to mark the end of a textbook flight. Within two hours, Wally and Tom were down safely in the Western Atlantic.

That left poor Frank and Jim up there all by themselves. By this point, the boredom onboard had become so overwhelming that the two had taken to singing a popular song of the era, Nat King Cole's cover of the Jim Reeves classic "He'll Have to Go" to one another, which featured the lines, "Put your sweet lips a little closer to the phone. Let's pretend that we're together, all alone …" A more appropriate lyric may well have been, "You better not shit unless your life depends on it." They were now at eleven days and counting and they still had three more days to go to fulfill their primary mission objective. Needless to say, morale inside the ship was not exactly at an all-time high. As Borman would later recall, "The last three days aboard Gemini VII were the toughest three days of my life just from the standpoint of just wanting to get out of something." He would nearly get his chance. On day twelve, a balky fuel cell caused enough concern that there was some serious thought given to bringing the guys down. By this point, they had nothing left to prove. Then the West Pointer in Borman kicked in. The mission, by damn, was for fourteen days. Anything less would not have been a fulfillment of his duty and in Frank's words, a "humiliation." Still, it took some reassurance from Kraft to pull Borman through until the end, a contribution which Frank later generously acknowledged. Despite having been pushed to their physiological limits, the crew stuck the landing a mile closer to the carrier than Schirra, winning their inflight bet. At 330 hours, 35 minutes and 1 second, Frank and Jim set an American endurance record that would not be broken until the Skylab program.

With the successful completion of the 76 mission, the Gemini program was now officially at the halfway point. Primary program objectives such as rudimentary EVA, long duration flight and rendezvous had been successfully accomplished and that was cause enough for some self-congratulatory celebration. The 76 crew members were rewarded with the obligatory citations, promotions and ticker-tape parades. Of the parades, none was more memorable than the one given to Borman in his hometown where the Tucson High Class of '46 turned out to let their conquering hero know that they hadn't forgotten him. Along the parade route, on a billboard perched high atop the Pioneer Hotel, they paid their tribute to Frank Borman. "Welcome Home Squarehead" was its proud proclamation.

WITH FIVE FLIGHTS REMAINING in the program, all of the remaining Mercury astronauts and New Nine commanders McDivitt and Borman had flown and were now being (or had already been) waved through to the Apollo program by Slayton. Starting with Gemini IX, every command thereafter would go to a Group 2 astronaut who had already flown second seat on a prior Gemini flight. That left Gemini VIII as the last mission to be commanded by a Group 2 rookie right out of the gate. The guy Deke chose for the task had flown the X-15 at Edwards and was already well known in both the test pilot and astronaut fraternities. Now the time had come for the rest of mankind to become acquainted with Neil Alden Armstrong.

# CHAPTER 5

# The Original
# "Houston, We Have a Problem"

G emini VIII would be the last American space mission to feature a rookie commander until Skylab 4. For that to happen, it took a deviation from Slayton's usual rotation of flight assignments combined with the occurrence of a horrific tragedy. As previously recounted, Deke essentially had to lay out the crew selections for the first four Gemini missions from scratch. After Shepard went down, that left Deke with only three viable Mercury astronauts to slot for the command of those missions. When Grissom was given command of Gemini 3 and brought along John Young, that shoved Tom Stafford into the backup pilot spot for that mission. Deke then assigned Wally to back up Gus, meaning that under the system Slayton had devised, Wally and Tom would skip two missions then become the prime crew for the rendezvous mission of Gemini VI. After McDivitt got tapped to be the first New Nine commander on Gemini IV, Borman and Lovell took the backup slots and later went prime on Gemini VII. According to the master plan, it would then follow that the backup crew for Cooper and Conrad's Gemini V mission—Neil Armstrong and Elliot See— would skip two flights and become the prime crew for Gemini VIII. However, a serious problem would emerge which caused Deke to have to deviate from the logical continuation of the flight rotation. That problem was named Elliot See. As Deke would later recount, "Of all the guys in the second group of astronauts, Elliot was the only one I had any doubts about." Not only did Deke have reservations about See's piloting skills (not "aggressive enough," too "old-womanish" Slayton recalled) but he further lamented the fact that Elliot wasn't even in particularly good physical condition. Because the Gemini VIII flight plan called for an extremely arduous EVA by the pilot, Deke feared that See simply would not be able to handle the level of physical exertion that functioning outside the spacecraft on the mission would require. Perhaps because he himself had endured the sting and humiliation of being selected as an astronaut and then being grounded before he ever flew in space, Deke refused to completely pass on Elliot and instead slotted him to command Gemini IX. Slayton then paired See with a highly regarded Group 3 astronaut named Charles "Charlie" Bassett who Deke deemed "strong enough to carry the two of them." It was a managerial choice that Slayton would later candidly characterize as "a bum decision" caused by the fact that he "had let myself get sentimental about Elliot." It also set in motion a chain of events that would end catastrophically for See and Bassett and which would cause ripples that would be felt in the overall program for years to come and which would impact flight assignments up to and including the initial lunar landing on Apollo 11.

In early 1966, as the training regimen for Gemini VIII was proceeding satisfactorily toward a scheduled launch date of March 16th, the prime and backup crews for Gemini IX had been assigned to fly from Houston to the McDonnell plant in St. Louis to conduct rendezvous training exercises using the on-site Gemini flight simulator at that facility. Flying NASA T-38 aircraft, the two crews left Houston early on the morning of February 28, 1966 with See and Bassett in the lead plane with backup commander Tom Stafford and Group 3 astronaut/backup pilot Eugene Cernan trailing them. As the two aircraft descended into Lambert Field in St. Louis next to the McDonnell facility, it became obvious very quickly that the four men were flying into weather conditions that were far worse than they'd anticipated. Years later, Stafford vividly described what happened next. According to Tom, both See and Stafford missed the middle marker (a flashing green light) on their initial approach and overshot the airport runway. Stafford quickly pulled up his wheels and aborted his landing and he fully expected See to do the same. For reasons that will never be known, Elliot kept his landing gear down and proceeded into a right bank then came back around and missed the runway again. Meanwhile, Stafford had ascended above the cloud cover and remained there in a holding pattern until his fuel situation became critical. When he was finally waved in by the control tower, Tom and Cernan had to descend through a snowstorm prior to landing. Once on the ground, the two were informed that Elliot had come in too low on his third approach and was then unable to regain altitude. At that point, he had pancaked the T-38 onto the roof of McDonnell Building 101—where the Gemini IX spacecraft was being assembled—and from there the airplane flipped into the parking lot and exploded upon impact. Both Elliot and Charlie were killed instantly. Of course, the news of the deaths of the two astronauts stunned the nation. Stafford would later recall that within NASA's New Nine, no member of the group took See's death any harder than his fellow civilian and Gemini V backup commander who was now currently in command of Gemini VIII.

Neil A. Armstrong was born on a farm near Wapakoneta, Ohio on August 5, 1930. Due to the fact that he would become the first human being to set foot on another celestial body, some stories about Armstrong's younger years have evolved into something approaching folklore. Still, there is no question that he was absolutely fascinated with aviation as far back as early childhood and that it was an abiding influence in his formative years. Later in life, Neil would recall a recurrent early childhood dream he'd had in which he floated above the ground. "I neither flew nor fell in those dreams," Neil remembered, "I just hovered." Academically, Neil was such a whiz that he was allowed to skip second grade in its entirety. Further setting himself apart, he took the model airplane gig of the era to a whole new level when he constructed a makeshift wind tunnel in the basement of the family's farmhouse. Tasking his siblings with an, "Okay … now go get Mom," Neil fired the contraption up for her and the damn thing shook the house so hard that it nearly blew their windows out into the corn-field. No wonder the kid made Eagle Scout.

Like Frank Borman, Neil earned a pilot's license before he was able to legally drive an automobile. Soon thereafter, he no doubt turned a few heads when he flew into West Lafayette, Indiana as a sixteen year old to preregister for classes at Purdue University. Neil entered Purdue as part of the U.S. Naval Aviation College Scholarship program. Per the terms of the so-called Holloway Plan, Neil would attend college for two years, then serve three on active duty and then come back and finish the last two years of college. Neil would eventually earn his B.S. from Purdue in aero-nautical engineering in January, 1955. In the middle of his Purdue experience, however, Armstrong earned his wings as a naval avi-ator and eventually flew 78 combat missions during the Korean War, the last of which was on March 5, 1952, still months before his twenty second birthday.

Following his graduation from Purdue, Armstrong joined the National Advisory Committee for Aeronautics (NACA) and had landed a test pilot job at Edwards by July, 1955. There, he would become one of a select few pilots to fly the legend-ary X-15, once taking the aircraft to an altitude of 207,500 feet. From there it was on to the New Nine where after See's death he would often be referred to as NASA's "only civilian pilot" giving the highly misleading impression that Neil had just sauntered out of the Pan Am terminal all suntanned in his blue and gold suit straight onto the NASA flight line. His sparkling résumé demonstrated that nothing could have been further from the truth and many of his fellow astronauts (none, however, with the last name "Shepard") considered Neil to be the best pilot at NASA despite the fact that he wasn't on active military duty at the time of his selection as an astronaut.

There was also no questioning Armstrong's nerve. On September 3, 1951, Neil was making a bombing run at 500 feet near Wonsan when a North Korean booby trap cable sliced off approximately six feet of his right wing. Neil was able to keep the plane level and stayed aloft long enough to eject far enough down the South Korean coast to avoid capture. Years later, in the leadup to Apollo 11, Neil was preparing for the lunar descent portion of the mission using a craft called the Lunar Landing Training Vehicle (LLTV). Dubbed "The Flying Bedstead" by the astronauts because of its ungainly appearance and balky controls, it was a notoriously difficult machine to fly. One sunny day while it wrestled with Neil during a particularly arduous run, the bedstead tried to turn Armstrong upside down which ultimately would have resulted in the vehicle piledriving him headfirst into the ground. With little more than a second to spare, Neil punched out with just enough altitude for his chute to open and deliver him to the ground in one piece. Group 3 astronaut Alan Bean, once he'd been informed of the incident, related that if something similar had befallen him he'd have regaled everyone within earshot—from atop a barstool—that the LLTV had just damn near killed him. Further, he fully expected to find Armstrong doing the same thing that day. Remarkably, when Bean finally located Neil, he was sitting in his office calmly finishing up some paperwork. Bean just laughed and shook his head in amazement. This guy just didn't rattle. It was a quality that would serve Armstrong well on Gemini VIII.

Chosen by Slayton to "replace" Elliot See in the pilot seat on Gemini VIII was Dave Scott, the first of the Group 3 astronauts after Bassett to be given a flight assignment. Even more impressive was that he was chosen to fly prime without ever having served on a backup crew. David Randolph Scott came into the world on June 6, 1932, the firstborn son of an Air Force general. Seemingly born to be a pilot, his middle name was taken from the airfield where his father was stationed on the date of his birth. Also, from early childhood, it was readily apparent that little Davy was fueled by a desire to gain his father's approval which eventually led to him becoming a pilot and joining the Air Force. A record-breaking swimmer while attending high school in Riverside, California, he received an athletic scholarship to the University of Michigan but remained there only one year before accepting an appointment to the U.S. Military Academy. By the time he got his Air Force wings in 1954, the Korean conflict had been suspended and Scott was stationed in Europe until 1960. Having been led to believe that the best path to test pilot school was to get a post-graduate degree, Dave obtained one from the Massachusetts Institute of Technology (MIT) in aeronautics and astronautics in 1962. Thinking he was headed to Edwards, he was mortified to find out that he had instead been tapped to be a professor at the newly-opened Air Force Academy in Colorado Springs. Determined not to let his flying career end in such a manner, Dave marched into the Pentagon one day and proceeded to schmooze a full-bird colonel who was so impressed by Scott's moxie that he personally arranged a change in Dave's orders and sent him to Edwards. It turned out to be a mutually beneficial decision when Dave won the best pilot award in his class which was presented to him by Chuck Yeager. From there, Scott was chosen for the Aerospace Research Pilot School at Edwards where he once cheated death in a spectacular crash of an F-104. In March, 1963, Scott applied to NASA and was accepted with the third group of astronauts in October of that year. As for Dave's selection to Gemini VIII, it would strain credulity to think that his physical prowess didn't have some influence on Slayton during the selection process given the rigors that were going to be required of the pilot on the flight—particularly the EVA which was going to be only the second time an American astronaut had ventured outside a spacecraft in flight. While he was not the athlete that Ed White was—no one in the astronaut corps could make that claim—Dave was as strong as he was agile and he could give Captain America a run for his money in the shallow end of a swimming pool. All those qualities were a must because the ultra-ambitious EVA planned for Gemini VIII wasn't going to be anything like the Gemini IV float-around that Ed had executed so flawlessly.

Picking up where the original Gemini VI flight plan left off, the primary mission objective of Gemini VIII would be to follow the Agena target vehicle into orbit, execute a rendezvous, keep station with it, then for the first time move in and physically dock with it. In addition to the explosion on the Gemini VI mission, there had been a number of development problems with the

Agena which had led NASA to consider just jamming the Agena docking collar onto the top of an Atlas rocket and sending it up as the target so that a simple docking could be achieved and the NASA brass could at least check that off their list of program objectives. Fortunately, NASA was able to get the Agena rocket mission-rated in time for Gemini VIII. As a result, another equally important task could be attempted—that of simultaneously being able to use the integrated systems of the Gemini spacecraft and the Agena rocket while docked to perform various maneuvers such as raising the altitude of the conjoined vehicles.

Every bit as ambitious as the vehicular flight plan was the EVA planned for Scott. On Gemini IV Ed White had gone out with only his chest pack oxygen supply and the hand-held zip gun maneuvering unit. On VIII, Scott would egress the spacecraft on a tether with a zip gun to help him maneuver himself to the bottom of the adapter section where a device called the Extravehicular Support Package (ESP, or more simply, "the backpack") was stowed. Scott would then strap on the backpack and switch his oxygen supply over to a longer tether. In theory, with the added oxygen supply and the additional length of tether, Scott would be able to stay out much longer than had White or Leonov (especially Leonov) and maneuver farther away from the Gemini spacecraft. While outside, Dave would remove a micrometeorite package from the Agena and use a power wrench in the weightless environment—all while being towed by the Gemini while tethered to it.

Scott trained assiduously for the EVA portion of the mission doing over 300 zero-G parabolas aboard the Vomit Comet and another 20 hours floating atop an oversized air hockey table using the zip gun to maneuver across the air-cushioned surface. Then there was the occasional comedy hour in the gym where Dave sweated and strained through all manner of weight training while Armstrong was perched atop a nearby stationary bike, dark socks accenting his NASA-issue gray sweatpants, pedaling just hard enough to keep the wheel turning, all the while exhorting, "You're doing well Dave...really well" without ever coming even remotely close to achieving perspiration. Scott graciously accepted Neil's explanation that he believed that every human being is only allotted a specific number of heartbeats in life and that Neil didn't intend to waste any of his on exercise. Well, that and the fact that Neil was his commander.

On the flight control side, the growing demands and the timeline of the impending Apollo program had finally forced Chris Kraft to bid a fond farewell to the Gemini program. That left only two fully trained flight control teams, one led by Kranz and the other by John Hodge. The two teams would alternate twelve hour shifts on Gemini VIII while Glynn Lunney and Cliff Charlesworth were each tasked by Kraft with assembling new flight control teams for future Gemini and Apollo missions. As for Hodge and Kranz, Kraft didn't mince words. "I'd trained them," he said, "and they were good." Predictably, Kraft's assessment was spot-on and it was a damn good thing because it wouldn't take long for his star pupils to get thrown to the wolves.

Approximately an hour and forty one minutes before the scheduled launch of Gemini VIII, the Atlas/Agena rumbled off Pad 14 and headed skyward. In a marked improvement over Gemini VI's Agena, the vehicle actually made it into Earth orbit without exploding. "It looks like we have a live one up there for you" was how Scott recalled Agena launch control's report to Gemini VIII. "Good show," Neil replied, "...We will take that one." At 10:41 a.m. EST, Gemini VIII cleared the launch tower and Hodge's crew down at Mission Control in Houston took over the flight from the Cape. At 4:11, Armstrong let loose with "Boy, oh boy! ...here we go." At 6:13, the Titan had finished its tasks and Neil and Dave were locked into an orbit 140 miles high.

With the initial hurdles cleared and both vehicles now functioning properly in orbit, Armstrong's next major task was to begin the process of trying to catch up to the target vehicle. Neil began the sequence at 1:34:00 with a five second burst of the spacecraft's forward OAMS thrusters to slow the vehicle into a position where its orbital inclination matched up precisely with that of the Agena. Over the course of the next four or so hours, Armstrong would make another eight subtle maneuvers to synchronize the

Gemini spacecraft's orbit with that of his target. At 3:43:59, Neil reported a "Solid radar lock" on the Agena and that they were 158 miles from it. At 4:47:33 Armstrong called out a "Solid visual on the Agena at 56 miles." At 5:50:25 Scott reported that Gemini VIII had braked and was 168 feet from the target. Three minutes later Dave called out "Outstanding job, coach.", a nickname he had given to his commander during training—perhaps while Armstrong was hurrahing his efforts during Neil's non–exertion atop the exercise bike. At 5:56:23 Neil confirmed, "We're station-keeping on the Agena at 150 feet." The second rendezvous of the Gemini program and all human spaceflight had been achieved.

At this stage of the game on Gemini VI, Wally and Tom were tasked with maintaining stationkeeping with VII for a few orbits to prove that it could be done, particularly through the nighttime cycles, and then back away and come home. Neil and Dave were now charged with a very different task which was to close the nose end of the Gemini in toward the docking adapter on the Agena and then physically join the two vehicles together. But they weren't going to move in just yet. At 6:00:43 Scott, after giving their target a once-over reported, "The Agena looks in fine shape." Meanwhile, Armstrong appeared to be having a ball just flying the Gemini, reporting "Man, it flies easy" and "This stationkeeping, there's nothing to it." Finally, at 6:32:31, Armstrong called "We're sitting about two feet out… We'll go ahead and dock." At 6:33:52, Armstrong cried out, "Flight, we are docked" followed by either he or Scott stating "It's a real smoothie." Rogering congratulations from Mission Control, Scott at 6:34:07 stated, "You couldn't have the thrill down there that we have up here" and Neil, a few seconds later followed with, "The Agena was very stable and at the present time we are having no noticeable oscillations at all."

As fate would have it, Neil and Dave would have precious little time to savor the smoothie, the thrill and especially the lack of noticeable oscillations. Because of the Agena explosion on Gemini VI and the other development problems with the vehicle, there was not a soul in Mission Control or at any of NASA's other tracking stations that was not absolutely as leery as hell of the

Agena. At 6:55:38, Tananarieve Capcom Jim Lovell radioed up the following ominous warning only minutes before that tracking station's Loss Of Signal (LOS) with the spacecraft, "If you run into trouble and the Attitude Control System in the Agena goes wild just send in the Command 400 to turn it off and take control with the spacecraft. Do you copy that?" To which Scott replied, "Roger, we understand!" At 7:02:08 Lovell reported Tananarieve LOS. Then as Chris Kraft would so succinctly put it, "They'd no more passed out of radio contact when all hell broke loose."

For the next fifteen minutes, while the docked Gemini/Agena flew over the Indian Ocean, it would be completely out of contact with any of NASA's tracking facilities on the ground. Accordingly, the only accounts of what happened during that span of time are those related by Neil and Dave themselves. After losing comm with Lovell, Neil and Dave had passed into a nighttime cycle. Further, because of the orientation of the Earth beneath them, it would only be possible to communicate with Houston for three five minute periods every ninety minutes via NASA's tracking stations aboard the ships Coastal Sentry Quebec (CSQ) off the coast of China and Rose Knot Victor (RKV) off the southeast coast of South America. In other words, these guys were way out on a limb when Dave glanced over at Neil's control panel at the "8-Ball" attitude indicator and noticed that it had registered an anomaly. Scott immediately informed Armstrong, "Neil, we're in a bank." In fact, the 8-Ball showed that they were in a 30 degree bank which meant that the spacecraft was, in aviation terms, in a roll. There are three basic descriptions of aircraft movements that translated to spacecraft: (a) "Pitch" which could be altered by the movement of the nose of the vehicle up or down; (b) "Yaw" which could be altered by movement of the nose left or right; and (c) "Roll" which meant that the craft was spinning. Further, right roll meant that the vehicle was spinning clockwise; left roll meant that it was spinning counterclockwise. Neil and Dave were spinning counterclockwise in a left roll. Armstrong then tried two things. First, he attempted to damp out the movement with the OAMS thrusters on the Gemini. That worked briefly but the roll started back up again. With Lovell's warning still fresh in mind and thinking, logically, that the problem was with the Agena, Neil then ordered Dave to turn off the Agena's attitude control system. That maneuver also appeared to work and the craft steadied for approximately four minutes. It was at that point that Kraft's vision of hell began to take shape. The roll started again only this time with increased intensity. Neil and Dave switched on and then again shut down the Agena but now the docked vehicles were experiencing malfunctions in pitch and yaw as well. It was, as Scott later described, like "Peering out from inside an enormous and intricate silver baton which had been hurled through space by a cosmic majorette." The immediate problem was that the docking collar holding the two vehicles together wasn't designed for them to be baton-tossed by a cosmic majorette and there was a very real danger that the mechanism would break. That, in turn, would wreak absolute havoc on the flight paths of both the Gemini and the Agena and perhaps even cause them to intersect. Obviously, that would have resulted in a catastrophe. Neil knew he had to get away from the Agena on his own terms if he was going to have any shot at saving Gemini VIII, Dave and himself. While Scott deftly remembered to transfer all Agena controls to the ground, Neil took his last best shot at steadying the docked vehicles. Unfortunately, that effort was unsuccessful.

With a "Rog undock, NOW!" from Neil, Dave hit the undock button on his side of the control panel while Neil yanked the Gemini up and away from the tumbling Agena. Now perhaps they were safe. Or not. Because the Gemini's OAMS fuel quantity was reading down on the gauges—*way* down—prior to undocking, Neil and Dave had begun to suspect that the real culprit in all this might be a thruster malfunction on the Gemini rather than some unknown problem with the Agena. That suspicion was about to be confirmed with a really hard kick in the pants from their spacecraft. Once clear of the Agena, Gemini VIII started rolling left again and, as Gene Kranz pointed out, "At undocking the Gemini spacecraft had shed almost half its mass (i.e. the Agena). Now, as a much lighter spacecraft, the effect of the continuously firing

Gemini thrusters virtually doubled." As a result, the Gemini was spinning twice as fast as before. In this centrifugal whirlygig the bad thing that was going to happen first was that their vision was going to start to degrade. So now Neil and Dave were in deep shit. Like up to their helmet latches deep and, if they didn't get the problem unwound within the next few minutes, the shit was only going to get exponentially deeper. Much longer than that and NASA was going to have two dead astronauts continually circling the Earth with absolutely no way to bring them back down again and without ever knowing or even being able to ascertain later what had killed them in the first place.

At 7:17:15, CSQ Capcom James Fucci got reacquisition of signal on Gemini VIII but was confused when his indicators showed that the vehicles were undocked and that the Gemini was rolling. Scott called down, "We have serious problems here. We're …we're tumbling end over end up here and we can't turn anything off… we've disengaged from the Agena." At this stage of the game, while the possibility of colliding with the Agena (and its 8000 pounds of rocket fuel) had not yet abated, the more pressing concern was that the stresses of the violent movements of the spacecraft might actually cause the Gemini to fly apart. It was at this point that Armstrong made the instinctive decision that would save Gemini VIII and both of their lives. Looking at Scott, Neil said, "All we've got left is the Reentry Control System" to which Scott replied, "Press on." At 7:20:05, Scott called the CSQ and advised, "We're regaining control of the spacecraft on RCS direct." By tapping into the RCS fuel system and engaging the thrusters in the nose of the spacecraft that were supposed to be used only during ret-rofire, Neil had been able to stabilize the Gemini VIII spacecraft and save both of their asses. However, mission rules dictated that once the RCS had been activated the flight had to immediately be aborted. At 7:22:41, Armstrong called down half-heartedly that they were only using one of the two RCS fuel rings (i.e. "Guys, we're conserving fuel, could you please not abort us? … pretty please?"). But the jig was up. There was no way in hell Hodge wasn't going to bring them down under these circumstances. Not on his first shift as a prime flight director and especially not with Kraft's eyeballs boring a hole into the back of his skull from the back row of Mission Control. The only choice left for Hodge at this point was which recovery zone he was going to bring them down in. Hodge didn't blink. Gemini VIII would come down on its seventh orbit in the South China Sea with recovery to be made by the destroyer USS Leonard Mason. At 7:38:27, any lingering hope aboard Gemini VIII was dashed when Hawaii Capcom instructed, "Get into retro attitude as soon as possible." Neil and Dave were coming down—now.

Of course, there were still concerns in both Mission Control and aboard the spacecraft. Mission Control's preoccupation with the location of the Agena over the next couple of hours was a pretty good indication that they were not entirely convinced that Gemini VIII wouldn't collide with it. Thankfully, that concern proved to be overblown. Also, neither Neil or Dave was particularly happy about the remoteness of the chosen site for the splashdown with Neil stating at 9:38:02 "I hate to land way out in the wilderness." And, of course, Neil was disappointed that Dave's EVA training, which he had so diligently overseen, had all been for naught.

Having seen Hodge have his ass so excruciatingly dragged through the keyhole during his first-ever shift on console as a prime flight director, Kranz bailed him out an hour early. Had the mission gone off as scheduled, Kranz and his guys would have been on duty for the splash and recovery anyway. Because of the abort, Scott had to purge all rendezvous data from the memory of the onboard digital computer and then enter seventy precise keystrokes for the reentry program. If he screwed up, he and Neil might well end up one tree over from Voskhod 2. Thankfully, Dave got it right and at 10:04:07, the retrofire sequence began with Scott confirming that all "four retros fired" twenty four seconds later. At 10:40:09, Dave confirmed that they were coming down over water. Whatever happened next, at least they wouldn't end up as a pair of imperialist lawn jockeys in Mao Zedong's front yard. Two minutes later, Gemini VIII was floating safely in the South China Sea. Their overshoot of the primary recovery zone set a record that no other American spacecraft would ever come close to breaking.

Of course, with the improvised reentry, it took the recovery forces awhile to get there during which time Armstrong and Scott had to endure heaving seas, noxious fumes from the heat shield and the stench of each other's vomit. Then, once the Mason arrived three hours after splashdown, the heavy swells caused the spacecraft (with Neil and Dave still inside) to be repeatedly banged against the side of the ship while being winched up out of the water. The final indignity for Scott, West Pointer to the core, was that he had to be plucked out of the spacecraft by the arm—by a lowly Navy swabbo.

In the aftermath of the flight, Scott's presence of mind to return control of the Agena to the ground was widely praised as it allowed the Agena flight control team to test the vehicle thoroughly, putting it through ten maneuvers over the next two days during which they absolved the vehicle from any suspicion of playing a role in the near disaster of the flight. As to the Gemini VIII spacecraft, it was hauled back to the McDonnell plant where it was definitively determined that OAMS thruster #8 was the culprit in that its valves unintentionally remained continuously open due to an electrical short. The problem was corrected with a redesigned switch inside the spacecraft.

As for Neil and Dave, they were alive and well and ready to move back into Deke's line for future flight assignments after the near-tragic ending of Gemini VIII. Although Scott's contributions and those of Mission Control and the recovery forces on down the line should never be undersold, it was Armstrong, with his decision to go to RCS direct during the crisis, who essentially saved the mission (Dave Scott himself has graciously acknowledged as much) and perhaps the entire space program as well. It was a feat that Slayton would not forget and in the coming years when he was confronted with the decision to name Armstrong to the command of what could potentially be the first lunar landing mission, Deke did not hesitate to pull the trigger. As it stood, two primary program objectives had been achieved by Gemini VIII with the rendezvous and docking with the Agena. It would be the task of Gemini IX to demonstrate whether rendezvous, docking and EVA could all successfully be accomplished during one mission.

**Gemini 3 Launch** "You're on your way, Molly Brown"

# Crew Photos

**Gemini 3** Gus Grissom and John Young

**Gemini IV** Ed White and Jim McDivitt

**Gemini V** Pete Conrad and Gordo Cooper

**Gemini VI** Tom Stafford and Wally Schirra

**Gemini VII** Jim Lovell and Frank Borman

**Gemini VIII** Dave Scott and Neil Armstrong

**Gemini IX** Tom Stafford and Gene Cernan

**Gemini X** John Young and Mike Collins

**Gemini XI** Dick Gordon and Pete Conrad

**Gemini XII** Buzz Aldrin and Jim Lovell

Chris Kraft

Gene Kranz

Deke Slayton

Alan Shepard

CHAPTER 6

# These Boots
# Ain't Made for Walkin'

**B**y early 1966, the American space program was exceptionally well-positioned. With the unequivocal commitment to
the LOR master plan having been made, the Gemini program was
proving increment by increment that the requisite capabilities for
taking that plan from the drawing board into space were attainable.
Further, the hardware that would carry Americans to the moon
was already well into development and the crews for the first missions of what had come to be known as Project Apollo had been
selected and had begun to train in earnest for those missions. Still,
despite all the progress that had been made in the overall program
since Al Shepard's maiden flight back in May of 1961, there was a
question that gnawed at the mind of every NASA employee when
that person's head hit the pillow each night: What the hell were the
Russians up to?

Despite the Soviet Union's absolute devotion to veiled secrecy
in nearly all matters pertaining to the State, one fact that simply
could not be concealed from the West was that Nikita Khrushchev
had been deposed on October 14, 1964. Whether it was the humiliation that had been inflicted upon him as the result of the Cuban
Missile Crisis fiasco that he had orchestrated, his embarrassing
devotion to provocative rhetoric and bullying, matters not known
or some combination of all of those factors, Khrushchev's sup-
porters inside the Kremlin had turned on him. In an unusual and
surprising display of magnanimity from the Soviet government of

the era, the outgoing chairman had somehow managed to avoid being treated to a pair of KGB bullets in the back of his skull. Instead, he had been declared a nonentity and was banished to his dacha where he would live out the remainder of his life under constant surveillance during what was essentially a prolonged house arrest. Whether his unwavering commitment to the Soviet space program had been entirely motivated by geopolitics or not, the loss of Khrushchev did not bode particularly well for those associated with it. However, it was the loss of another man, one whose identity was entirely unknown to any of the western intelligence agencies, that would constitute a blow far more devastating to the Soviet quest to be first to the moon than the exile of Nikita Khrushchev.

Sergei Pavlovich Korolev was born in the Ukraine on January 12, 1906. Tapped in the early 1930s to work in Russia's fledgling rocket program, Korolev had been implicated by colleagues as a subversive during Stalin's great purge and had been tried and sentenced to death. Eventually, he would succeed in having his sentence reduced but not before spending prolonged periods of time in some of the Mother Country's finest gulags. That, in turn, would have a ruinous effect on his health in the decades to come. Following the surrender of Hitler's armies in 1945, Stalin made development of rocket and missile technology a Soviet state priority. Korolev was then chosen to supervise the work of Russia's cache of captured German rocket scientists and engineers—much in the same manner as Wernher Von Braun on behalf of the United States in postwar New Mexico. From there, Korolev went on to oversee the development of the clustered engine R-7 booster which would lift the Sputniks and Gagarin's Vostok 1 into orbit.

Recognizing his immense value and fearing that the Americans might attempt to assassinate him if his true identity was revealed, Korolev was identified to the world by the Soviet Union's propaganda ministry only as "The Chief Designer." Alexei Leonov, the Soviet spacewalker on Voskhod 2, noted that he and his fellow cosmonauts, even those that actually knew The Chief Designer's name, never dared to address him by it. Rather, they addressed him by his official title, "SP", or simply "The Chief." Leonov, himself a socialist icon with a status akin to that of Gagarin, said simply that Korolev "was treated like a God" within the Soviet space agency. Unfortunately, The Chief's godlike status did not immunize him from the physical maladies of a mortal earthling and on December 3, 1960, shortly before his fifty-fifth birthday, Korolev suffered a heart attack. During his convalescence, a kidney ailment believed to have been caused by his years in the gulags was detected. At that time, his physicians warned him to dial back his workload or risk severe consequences to his health. Korolev, however, had become convinced that Khrushchev's only interest in his space program was its propaganda value and that his premier might simply end it if it ever appeared that the Americans were forging ahead in the race to the moon. So, rather than easing off the accelerator, Korolev chose instead to mash it to the floorboard. That decision would prove to be disastrous and, on January 16, 1966, the space race ended for Sergei Korolev on a Soviet operating table. The Chief may have bled out during surgery to remove a cancerous tumor in his stomach or a procedure to remove a polyp from his colon or maybe it had been a hemorroidectomy gone horribly awry. Characteristically, the Soviets would never confirm or deny any of the rumors. At least they had the decency to inter Korolev's cremated remains in an honored resting place in the Kremlin Wall. It was a far more dignified end than the one Khrushchev had gotten.

Now, as Gemini began to truly stretch its legs and explore the limits of its capabilities, the Soviets had banished their bombastic impressario of a premier who had demanded the Russia-first space spectaculars to oblivion and the enigmatic rocket and engineering genius who had somehow made them a reality was dead. Would it be possible for the new masters of the Kremlin and the new Chief Designer to pick up where their predecessors had left off? Of course, only time would tell. But with the Soviet rocket program's capacity for heavy lifting capability, they would always have a chance to complete a Hail Mary pass and put the United States back in second place as they had so many times before. Because of that fact, the Russians would always have a puncher's chance to win this fight and it would not end definitively in a U.S. victory until an American astronaut put his boot down in the lunar soil. Of course, for an American astronaut to take that step, it had to be proven that he (and in 1960s' America it was going to be a he) could survive outside the confines of the spacecraft. That capability would have to be proven by what the guys who wore the pocket protectors in Mission Control called Extra Vehicular Activity or EVA (pronounced EE-VEE-AY). The American public would come to characterize the activity as "spacewalking" which would turn out to be about as bad a misnomer as any they could possibly have chosen.

Although the press had romanticized the EVA concept and the American public had gone fairly goofy about the idea, there was no mistaking the fact that there were more than a few steely-eyed missilemen in Mission Control who thought that EVA was about as bad as a bad idea could get. Aside from the fact that the whole thing just felt like some Lost in Space science fiction bull-shit, Ed White's difficulty in getting back inside Gemini IV had not been lost on those guys. Neither was the difficulty that Jim and Ed had with the latches on Ed's hatch door and with just getting the damn thing to close in the first place. Moreover, the reasoning and the stated purposes behind the whole Gemini EVA concept just didn't hold water with some of the skinny tie guys. NASA's primary justifications for risking EVA, in no particular order of emphasis, went something like this: (1) Well, we have to see if men can live and work in space in order to see if they can live and work on the moon; (2) We have to test the integrity of the EVA suit in the vacuum of space; (3) We have to see if an astronaut could make an emergency repair to the exterior of a spacecraft; and (4) We have to be able to do an emergency transfer of the Lunar Module (LM) crew to the Command and Service Module (CSM) in case the docking mechanism between the two vehicles fails during lunar orbit rendezvous. EVA's opponents had valid coun-terarguments to every single point. As to (1), it was more than a little absurd because the conditions which an astronaut would face outside during a weightless Gemini EVA were radically different than those he would encounter during an EVA on the surface of the moon. It had long ago been proven that the moon has a gravity field that is approximately one-sixth that of Earth. That meant that any organism or object that landed on the lunar surface would weigh approximately one-sixth of what it weighed on Earth. But more importantly, there was *gravity*. That meant that when an astronaut put his boots on the surface they would stay on the surface. So would any other piece of equipment that he chose to bring along. Accordingly, no amount of activity or training outside an orbiting Gemini spacecraft in zero-G could possibly have any practical application or translation to a lunar surface EVA; As to (2), pressure suits had been vacuum tested and in use in high altitude airplane flight for more than a decade and had been proven to be extremely reliable. Even if there was some need to test them in the vacuum of space all the crew had to do was pressurize the suits, depressurize the cabin and open the hatch. The astronaut on the side of the open hatch could even stand up in his seat, if that was deemed necessary, but there sure as hell wasn't any reason for him to leave the relative safety of the spacecraft—especially not while attached to a tether that he could easily get tangled around himself or the ship; As to (3), any damage to the exterior of a spacecraft in flight serious enough to require an astronaut to go outside to repair it would probably kill the crew in the first place; and As to (4), in the highly unlikely event that such a maneuver was ever necessitated, a spacewalk from the LM to the CSM would not be tethered. Rather, it would be an ass-over-teakettles shitstorm that the LM astronauts would simply have to try to survive as best they could under the circumstances as they existed at that time.

One of the most formidable individuals in the group that was dead set against EVA was White Team (Kranz's) flight controller John Llewellyn. In later years, Llewellyn would say, "If it was up to me, we wouldn't do EVAs. Because if you got out, you might not come back. It was a dangerous thing to do." His fears would almost prove to be prophetic on a few occasions—particularly during Gemini IX. Interesting guy, Llewellyn. There were three things about him that really stood out. First, he was a Marine who had been in combat in Korea. Second, he practiced judo with Gene Kranz who was built like a gunsafe with arms and, finally, during a contentious after-hours meeting between some astronauts and flight controllers prior to Gemini 3, John had squared off with Al Shepard, snarling at the Freedom 7 hero, "I got more Purple Hearts than you'll ever see in your lifetime, you SOB." When it was all over, Shepard knew way better than to put an alligator in John Llewellyn's swimming pool. A couple of years later, during the post-Gemini VII liftoff turnaround for Gemini VI, Llewellyn overslept the start of his shift. Upon arriving at the MSC, he discovered that some asshole had poached his assigned parking space. After circling the lot once in an unsuccessful search for another spot, he then drove his Triumph TR-3 straight up the sidewalk and parked right in front of building's main entrance for the rest of the day. Flight Directors Lunney and Hodge, concurring that John "needed to be taught a lesson," then decided to jerk his parking space. It only took until the next morning for them to discover that their disciplinary plan hadn't quite had the desired effect when they looked out their office windows and caught sight of Llewellyn galloping through the parking lot—on a horse. John then dismounted at the same entrance where he'd previously parked the TR-3 and used the bike rack as a hitchin' post. Not quite sure what the hell to do but pretty damned certain that they didn't want the lobby of the building to be permeated with the various odors capable of being produced by a horse, Lunney and Hodge quickly rescinded their parking ban while simultaneously figuring out that there are far more productive ways to use one's time in life than to spend it fucking with John Llewellyn.

Of course, Llewellyn and the rest of the anti-EVA contingent never really stood a chance that their position would be given a fair hearing. Not only had the Russians gone EVA but they had done it before we did. Now NASA—being NASA—had to prove not only that the United States could match the feat but somehow better it. Added to that was the fact that now the Air Force had gotten involved in the debate. In order to facilitate their own ambitions in the space race, the Air Force had developed a device which they had named the Astronaut Maneuvering Unit (AMU) at Wright-Patterson. The AMU consisted of a backpack-like device which contained its own thruster system and oxygen supply as well as its own tether—all of which were to be independent of the spacecraft's systems. The operational theory was that the pilot astronaut would egress the spacecraft on the ship's tether and make his way back to the adapter section on the bottom end of the bell-shaped ship. Once there, he would anchor himself using an exterior foothold, strap the gizmo on, disconnect the spacecraft tether and then perform EVA operations at the end of the AMU's longer 125 foot tether. The stated goals of the AMU project were to facilitate repair, rescue, crew transfer and "satellite inspection." By the mid-1960s, satellite technology was rapidly evolving and it was becoming clear that space was going to be the new high ground for intelligence gathering—perhaps even the conduct of warfare itself. Not about to let themselves get hemmed in by all those clammy-handed Kumbaya platitudes about how spaceflight could be of benefit to all mankind, the guys at the Pentagon with the stars on their shoulders wanted to find a way to exploit it to the military advantage of the United States. How wonderful a tool "satellite inspection" might turn out to be, particularly if an American astronaut on a spacewalk could perform a discreet "inspection" of or maybe even photograph the orbiting satellites of another country. Say, like Russia maybe.

With those clandestine objectives at stake along with all of the other perceived benefits that would (or at least could) flow from it, there was going to be a complex EVA on Gemini IX and it was going to involve testing of the AMU. The only real debate was how that testing was going to be conducted. An Air Force colonel named Daniel McKee was pushing hard for the AMU testing to be conducted while the astronaut was untethered from the spacecraft. With typical Cold War fervor, perhaps he felt that the potential for launching NASA's first permanent human satellite was worth the risk. Fortunately, the NASA brass did not and diplomatically but firmly notified McKee and his Air Force cronies that under no circumstances would they even consider sending an astronaut outside untethered at this stage of the program.

As to Gemini IX's other mission objectives, rendezvous and docking maneuvers would be at the forefront. On the rendezvous side, the previous successful operations of both 76 and Gemini VIII had each been accomplished during the spacecraft's fourth orbit after launch. Gemini IX would attempt to shorten that to what mission planners called M=3 or an initial rendezvous during the third orbit. Then, Stafford would dock and undock the spacecraft and pull away for two additional rendezvous attempts with the final one having Tom conduct the maneuver while coming down from a *higher* orbit above the Agena to simulate a rescue in lunar orbit by the CSM should the LM not be able to reach its target altitude after blasting off the surface of the moon. Along with the rendezvous, docking and EVA/AMU objectives, there was the standard menu of medical and photographic "experiments." The purpose of the photography was to test the high resolution capabilities of the equipment as much as to obtain the photographs themselves. Still, rendezvous, docking, photographic experiments and even a "standard" EVA had all been done before. Where NASA, the Soviets and the rest of the world were really going to focus their attention was on the spaceman with that Buck Rogers jetpack strapped to his back out there floating 125 feet away from the spacecraft. Which poor rookie was gonna draw the short straw on that one?

Eugene Andrew "Gene" Cernan was born on March 14, 1934 in Depression-era Chicago. As a boy, he watched World War II newsreels at his local theater and had become enamored with the idea of becoming a "fighter pilot." For whatever reason, for young Gene being a fighter pilot came to mean flying off of and landing on aircraft carriers. That, by definition, meant naval aviation. Following a stellar academic performance in high school, Gene chased his dream to Purdue University which, due to its superior engineering schools, was rapidly becoming a virtual astronaut pipeline. There he would graduate one year behind Neil Armstrong with the Class of 1956. A year earlier he had taken his first airplane ride which fortuitously turned out to be everything he'd hoped it would be. In 1958, Gene achieved his lifelong dream when he earned his carrier qualifications and became "a real naval aviator." In 1961, the Navy offered him a deal whereby he could attend the Naval post-graduate school while continuing to fly jets. Two years later, he earned a master's degree in aeronautical engineering. While pondering his next move, Cernan was stunned when he got word that the Navy, with no input from him whatsoever, had put his name up for consideration by NASA. He was probably even more surprised when NASA selected him as a Group 3 astronaut.

By his own admission, Gene at first felt like NASA's "Imposter Astronaut" and he unashamedly (and uncharacteristically for an astronaut) confessed that Al Shepard was his hero. Hell, he'd even asked the Mercury guys for their autographs when he first arrived in Houston. Gene was absolutely delighted to be assigned with Tom Stafford on the backup crew for Gemini IX because that meant if he didn't up and screw the pooch he would likely fly before Gemini was scheduled to end and thereby position himself for consideration for an Apollo flight. Further, Gene felt it was "an honor" to be backing up Charlie Bassett even though Charlie was a fellow Group 3 astronaut and a close friend. Then St. Louis happened and Stafford and Cernan went from being a backup crew to having a launch date in ten weeks. As to the crewmates, Slayton had once again done his homework on the compatibility scale. Where Stafford was reserved and economical in matters of speech, Geno was as articulate as hell and just as loquacious and there was damn near nothing that he wouldn't talk—and then talk some more—about, and while he was usually delightful, there were occasions when he went too far and had to be encouraged by Slayton and others at NASA to just shut the fuck up particularly if there were people with television cameras and notebooks around.

Seventy eight days after the crash in St. Louis, Tom and Gene sat patiently atop their Titan awaiting the launch of their Agena target vehicle off Pad 14. Both were naturally pleased when the rocket lifted off smoothly and climbed along its programmed trajectory. Then, without warning, the Atlas went hard over and the rocket blew itself up. Stafford's encyclopedic array and creative use of profanity were already becoming the stuff of legend throughout NASA. Back in Mission Control after the Atlas explosion, Gilruth winced and asked Kraft, "What do you suppose Stafford is saying about now?" Kraft immediately replied, "I don't know but you can bet that it isn't 'Aw shucks.'" Gilruth would've won that bet. It also had not gone unnoticed at the Cape that Stafford had now been sitting on the pad twice (previously on Gemini VI) when an Atlas/Agena target vehicle had blown itself to bits. That night an Air Force lieutenant colonel working at the Cape composed a verse in Stafford's honor. "I think that I shall never see," he wrote, "an Agena out in front of me." As the next Agena on the production line was slotted for Gemini X, his words were as prophetic as they were poetic, and, if Gemini IX was to proceed as scheduled, NASA would have to improvise.

Ever since the Agena failure on Gemini VI had caused NASA to have to shitcan the flight plan for that mission and because Agena rockets didn't grow on trees, the agency had been toying with ideas for a cheaper and more reliable (but mostly a cheaper) alternative to the Agena. What NASA eventually settled on was a hybrid contraption called the Augmented Targeting Docking Adapter (ATDA) which was essentially an Agena docking mechanism (minus the rocket, of course) which would be mated to the top of an Atlas rocket. Covering the docking mechanism was a protective shroud to shield it from the aerodynamic stresses of launch. Once the vehicle was in orbit, the shroud would detach leaving the mechanism open for docking operations with the Gemini spacecraft. Because there was no rocket engine on the ATDA, there would be no maneuvering of the conjoined vehicles but at least docking could be attempted provided Tom and Gene could find it up there.

On June 1, 1966, the ATDA was lofted into space from Pad 14 and this time Gemini IX's target vehicle actually attained orbit. But before the champagne could be uncorked, telemetry signals from the ATDA indicated that there was a potentially serious problem. Although Mission Control couldn't be absolutely certain without visual confirmation, their data appeared to indicate that the protective shroud covering the ATDA had failed to detach. Because NASA considered the three scheduled rendezvous maneuvers and Cernan's EVA on the AMU to be imperative mission and program objectives regardless of whether docking was possible, there would be no automatic scrub of Gemini IX. Tom and Gene would simply have to go up and take a look. Mission Control could then decide how to proceed based upon what the crew saw. So the countdown proceeded and everything was a go until T minus three minutes at which time the Titan abruptly refused to accept data from Mission Control. Kranz's guys furiously worked the problem in an effort to stay within the launch window but ultimately there had to be a scrub. By now, Stafford had been up and down the gantry elevator so many times that Guenter Wendt and his White Room crew had dubbed Tom "The Mayor of Pad 19." The taciturn Oklahoman wasn't even the slightest bit fucking amused.

Two days later, they'd try it again and on June 3, 1966, Tom and Gene suited up for a third time and made their way back to the launch complex where they were confronted with what Cernan would later term some more "grim" NASA humor. On the way out to the pad, Deke handed them a baton-sized cardboard cutout of a giant match for them to use to light the rocket if all else failed. Then, a guy Cernan described as "some smartass" had hung a sign on the door of the gantry elevator stating that the down capability of the lift had been disabled. Then there was the sign from their backup crew, Jim Lovell and Buzz Aldrin, over the hatch which read:

> We were kidding before
> But not anymore
> Get your ... uh ... selves into space
> Or we'll take your place.
> Jim and Buzz

That last part elicited a wry smile from Gene as he thought to himself that it would be a "cold day in hell" before Buzz Aldrin took his seat on Gemini IX. Unfortunately, that sign hanging on the hatch would not even come close to pissing Gene off as badly as some of the additional things Buzz would say and do before Gemini IX splashed down three days from now.

As it turned out, Tom and Gene would not need Deke's match and at 7:39:33 Houston time Gemini IX roared to life. Once safely in orbit, the crew's attention had to immediately shift to the first rendezvous sequence which, if it came off as planned, would catch them up to the ATDA on the spacecraft's third orbit. At this stage of the game Mission Control was well-versed in the art and science of rendezvous and they guided Gemini IX up perfectly to the target vehicle. Now it was time to determine if the telemetry from the ATDA which they had received two days prior was accurate. At 4:10:53, Stafford delivered the anticipated bad news with, "Would you believe that there's still a nose cone on that rascal?" to which Cernan replied, "There can't be … can there?" Indeed there was. Twenty two minutes later, after closing to within three feet of the ATDA, Stafford uttered the words that the press would use to define the mission, "It looks like an angry alligator out there rotating around." An angry alligator was not what Mission Control or the crew had bargained for and the implications were as clear as glass. As long as the protective shroud remained in place covering the ATDA, there would be no docking maneuvers on Gemini IX. The question then became whether or not there was anything Mission Control or the crew could do to rectify the situation. Kranz's first thought was to have the crew back off and have Mission Control "send a series of rapid attitude maneuver commands" up to the ATDA. Since the vehicle had some limited thruster capability, Kranz thought that firing a few bursts from the tiny rockets might shake the shroud loose. When the crew saw that the procedure just wasn't going to work, Stafford had the ground back off. By now, through visual inspection, Tom had determined that some lanyards which should have been wired to disconnect at the appropriate time once the ATDA reached orbit had been *taped* down prior to launch. It was later discovered that a Douglass Aircraft technician whose job it was to connect the lanyards was called away prior to the launch because his wife was about to give birth. On his way out the door, he had advised a McDonnell technician to "secure the disconnect lanyards." Seeing the wires hanging out and not knowing what the hell to do with them (and apparently being too thick-headed to actually ask someone) the McDonnell guy just hauled out a roll of duct tape and, well, there you have it. With that option now entirely off the table, Stafford got something of a wild hair up his ass and suggested that he simply drive up to the alligator and give it a nudge with the nose of the spacecraft and try to knock the shroud loose. In Mission Control, Kranz must have thought Stafford's oxygen supply was running thin given that—aside from fire—the worst thing that can happen in space is to have two vehicles collide with each other. Even if the idea had had any sort of merit both the OAMS and RCS fuel rings were housed in the nose of the spacecraft and there was no way under any circumstances that possibly compromising either of those fuel supplies could be deemed an acceptable risk.

Considering the entire ATDA matter now closed, Kranz concluded his shift and then went home for supper and some fresh clothes before returning to his sleeping quarters at Mission Control. Before sacking out, he wanted to check in with Glynn Lunney one last time in the control room only to find Cliff Charlesworth sitting in Lunney's chair. After asking why the hell Lunney wasn't in Lunney's chair, Kranz was informed that Glynn had been called to a meeting with the brass to discuss "tomorrow's EVA." Kranz's head nearly split open as he shouted, "What EVA!?" As it would turn out, Buzz Aldrin had hauled off and thrown an enormous monkey wrench at the Gemini IX flight plan.

Taking the steps two at a time up to the ready room where the meeting was being held, Kranz was greeted with an eyeroll from Lunney the moment he burst through the door. After being informed by Lunney that the assembled brass had been prodded by Aldrin into considering having Cernan go EVA to detach the shroud, Kranz exploded with a response so livid that Chris Kraft actually had to exhort his protégé to get himself under control. According to Kranz, the primary—if not only—proponent of this kooky scheme was Aldrin. Apparently, Buzz had pitched the idea that Cernan should suit up and perform a completely unscheduled and unrehearsed spacewalk over to the alligator and snip the tape holding down the lanyards around the firing wires. Of course, Buzz had also apparently failed to take into consideration that if the shroud came flying off with any significant degree of force, it could knock Cernan unconscious and/or severely injure him. Even worse was the possibility that a jagged edge or a wire could puncture Cernan's suit which would set his blood to boiling and kill him instantly. No problemo, Buzz proclaimed with increasing adamance, because the potential rewards certainly outweighed any risk to *Cernan's* life. Then came the kicker. Buzz let 'em all know that by God if this were his flight, he'd be out there right goddamn now pulling the ripcord on a chainsaw if that's what it took to do his duty. Even after Kranz gave an impassioned response explaining why implementing Buzz's plan would essentially be the stupidest thing NASA had ever done, the brass incomprehensibly still wanted to go ahead with it.

While the debate continued to rage on the ground, Stafford and Cernan had continued with their day one mission objectives including the third and final rendezvous from above the ATDA. Now the call had to be made and, as fate would have it, neither Aldrin, Kranz or anyone else in Mission Control would make it. Having eyeballed the alligator and being able to visualize firsthand all the different ways it could kill Cernan, Stafford as mission commander made the final decision. His call was as unceremonious as the man himself. "No way" Tom Stafford told them.

That was the end of the alligator EVA debate while the crew was in flight but it was hardly the end of the controversy. As was evidenced by his reaction to the hatch poem, Cernan's animosity toward his backup pilot was already beginning to boil over. To a degree it was unavoidable. After all, Buzz was a West Pointer, an Air Force pilot and a Phi Beta Kappa. Gene was Annapolis down to the anchor embroidered on his jockstrap, a naval aviator and not a Phi Beta Kappa. In a remarkably candid admission years later, Cernan stated that to do the job an astronaut had to be a little arrogant, perhaps even to the point of thinking himself to be invincible and bulletproof. And Lord knows there is nothing that grates at a guy like that more than another guy in the room that he believes is even more arrogant than he is. When, in addition to all that, Cernan found out that Aldrin had dared to Monday-morning quarterback his mission to the NASA brass, Geno was so fucking furious that he wanted to rip Buzz's throat out. For his part, Buzz just couldn't understand what Gene's problem was. With a tone-deaf imperiousness worthy of Sir Bernard Law Montgomery, Buzz thought it was his *duty* to point out what others lacked in ability, competence and/or courage. After all, if he didn't, how else were they to know if they were untalented, incompetent or cowardly? By letting them know, Buzz reasoned, he might actually help some of them find a way to overcome their deficiencies. Gee whiz, anyone could see that, right? Well, perhaps, but Buzz hadn't done himself any favors with Cernan and a whole bunch of other people at NASA by the time Gemini IX hit the water.

After completing the rendezvous maneuvers on day one, Stafford and Cernan were to then proceed with the AMU EVA on day two. As it had turned out, Tom and Gene had bitten off one hell of a chunk on the first day. Stafford informed the ground that both he and Gene were "pretty well bushed" and that it was against his better judgment to proceed with the EVA as scheduled. Accordingly, day two would be dedicated to the now mundane Gemini tasks of medical and photographic experiments. Further, with no way to fix the ATDA and with no type of docking maneuvers possible, there was no way in the world that either Stafford or Cernan wanted Gene to get out of the spacecraft anywhere in the vicinity of the alligator. It was time to move on but a couple of minutes after Stafford's ATDA EVA scrub decision Cernan, maybe grasping at a final straw or perhaps looking to have it on record that he was willing to do whatever it took to fix the alligator, made sure to ask Capcom Neil Armstrong over an open comm link if Mission Control had any recommendation to fix the ATDA. When Armstrong copied that they did not have any viable plan, Gene then relented while at the same time having made sure that he had stated very publicly that he was more than willing to do his part and that Mission Control's lack of a plan was the only thing holding his rarin'-to-go ass back.

On day three, of course, Geno would have the opportunity to demonstrate his mettle and prove once and for all that he was a real astronaut and not just an imposter. At 49:22:01 Cernan advised that he and Tom were opening the hatch and two minutes later he was standing upright in his seat with the upper half of his torso poking outside the ship. The first order of business was for Geno to deploy a handrail on the side of the ship while Stafford held onto his leg. Then, after snapping some pictures with the Hasselblad, Cernan would then be fed his spacecraft umbilical out the open hatch enabling him to start maneuvering back to the bottom of the adapter section which held the AMU in a concave recess inside the base. From this point forward, until he was able to finally reenter the spacecraft 128 minutes later, would transpire what Cernan himself would later characterize as "The spacewalk from hell."

Unfortunately for Geno, it was not any one aspect of what was to have been his singular contribution to Gemini IX that went south. Rather, it was a series of cascading failures that caused the exercise to degenerate into the bumbling nightmare that it turned out to be. At 49:33:56, only eleven minutes after hatch opening, came the first ominous sign when Cernan indicated that he needed a breather—and he hadn't yet gotten his feet all the way out of the ship. Once he did get outside, Gene would describe the experience as both "A lesson in Newton's Laws of Motion" and "wrestling an octopus." The problem was multi-faceted. First, because he had no suit thrusters or a zip gun like Ed White had on Gemini IV, he had no way to control his movement by engaging an exterior use of force. Anytime he tried to move himself, that movement would whipsaw through the umbilical and rock the spacecraft back and forth. Added to this was the fact that the handrail was inadequate to help Geno to steady himself as were the Velcro strips adhering to the outside of the ship. Without any way to anchor his torso, Cernan was exhausting himself just trying to stay still. Because the mission planners believed that the AMU thrusters posed a significant danger of burning through Gene's EVA suit, several layers of protective fabric had been added to it. As pressurization of the suits would cause the astronauts to blow up, in Cernan's words, "like a balloon in the Macy's parade" to begin with, the extra layers of insulation were now making it difficult for Gene to grip, move his shoulder joints and bend his wrists, elbows and knees. Still, Geno somehow managed to grapple with the exterior of the spacecraft and drag himself back to the base of the adapter section where the AMU awaited him. When he finally got there, one of the two exterior lights that were there to help him get the device on was not functioning. That, as it turned out, would be the least of Geno's problems. By now, his physical exertion while assembling the AMU was leading to bio-med sensor readings that the flight surgeon just didn't like. Foremost among them was the indication that Cernan's heart rate had exceeded 155 BPM and had touched 180. Then, at 50:30:09, came the beginning of the end, when Cernan called out, "Who said this visor wouldn't fog up?" Holy shit. Along with everything else, now his vision was compromised? Desperate, Cernan had pushed the tip of his nose up against the inside of his faceplate and rubbed it in a circular motion to clear a little peephole to see out. Then, at 50:59:29, Stafford reported to Hawaii Capcom that his comm link with Cernan had started to break up. Four minutes later, Stafford had seen and (not) heard enough and officially scrubbed the AMU EVA. Further, he ordered Gene to immediately get back on the spacecraft umbilical and then get his ass back to the hatch. Cernan did not even attempt to protest and merely offered a wistful apology to "everyone down there" through Capcom Neil Armstrong. With Stafford literally pulling him back toward the hatch by the umbilical, an exhausted and fogged over Cernan finally got there.

Now, the two of them were faced with what Cernan described as "putting a champagne cork back in a champagne bottle." At 51:27:33 Stafford reported they were having "a very big deal" getting the hatch closed. Because of the rigidity of Cernan's suit, he'd had to bend his knees underneath himself like a guy doing the limbo just to get into a position where they could physically close the hatch door. Enduring pain which he later described as "awful" and "excruciating," Cernan held the pose while Stafford helped him ratchet down the hatch to where it could not pop open again. Helmet to helmet inside the cabin, Stafford could not see Cernan's face through the foggy visor. When the spacecraft finally repressurized and ended Cernan's agony on the rack, he lifted his visor and Stafford could then see that Cernan's face was as pink as a cured ham. Violating just about every mission rule in the book, Stafford grabbed his water gun and sprayed it directly onto Cernan's face. Mercifully, at long last, the spacewalk from hell was finally over.

While Cernan had been laboring outside, Stafford suddenly harkened back to a conversation he'd had with Slayton shortly prior to his and Geno's first trip to Pad 19 on May 14th. Basically, Slayton had sat Stafford down while he was suiting up and informed Tom that NASA had instructed him that Tom had to bring Cernan's body back if Geno died outside on the EVA. Tom felt as if Slayton had hit him in the center of the forehead with a hammer. Essentially, NASA had told Deke to inform Tom that— because it would be bad PR for NASA to have a dead astronaut floating around up in Earth orbit—he'd have to risk his own life bringing back Gene's corpse. Since it would be impossible to get a dead (or even an incapacitated) astronaut back inside in that bloated suit, that meant Stafford would have to reenter depressurized with the hatch open pulling Cernan's dead body on a tether. Assuming the plasma from reentry didn't kill Tom (which was a longshot), he'd then have to hope that whatever was left of Cernan wouldn't get tangled up with the chutes when they were deployed. Then, if he made it to splashdown with the hatch open, he'd have to hope he didn't sink and/or drown before the recovery forces could get there. Given all the variables, Stafford was understandably noncommittal. Only after the flight was over did Stafford relate to Cernan the details of his conversation with Slayton. When asked by Cernan if Tom would really have cut him loose up there, Stafford replied as only Stafford could, "Geno, how could you give a shit? You're already dead." Luckily for them both and for all of NASA, Tom didn't have to make that call.

Still, they had to get back down. At 69:24:17, a confident Stafford called down and asked Kano Capcom to tell Captain Hartley to anchor the Wasp right on the landing point. At 71:46:44, the now familiar retrofire sequence began. At 72:12:00 Cernan commented on the fireball engulfing Gemini IX prompting him to opine after the flight that there are no atheists in foxholes or in spacecrafts going through reentry. They hit like a sledgehammer at 72:20:43. So hard, in fact, that an internal water line burst causing them to momentarily fear that they were sinking. Nothing—absolutely nothing—had come cheap on this mission. The same was true of the post-flight debriefing when Tom and Gene had to somehow explain to Slayton and Big Al exactly what in the world all had happened up there.

IN THE END, TOM and Gene came through the process unscathed. In short order, they got treated to the standard ticker-tape adulation accorded a NASA space hero—which was right up Geno's alley, in particular. In this battle with the Russians, the American public flat out didn't give a damn about failed mission objectives. You stick your head in the dragon's mouth and pull it back out before it gets bitten off and you're a movie star. Geno liked that part too. The press, however, was beginning to be a different matter. Gemini IX wasn't an epic clusterfuck, not by any stretch of the imagination. Some important mission objectives had been achieved and, more importantly, no one had died. Still, NASA's one docking out of the three scheduled to this point had ended in a near-tragic abort and when those things were added to the docking and EVA failures on this flight, the program seemed to be slipping—particularly when the recent failures were juxtaposed against the near flawlessness of the four missions up to 76. Might the press actually consider revoking the patriotic free pass which it had given NASA so far? To preclude that, things needed to go a lot more smoothly on Gemini X. John W. Young, Gus's sidekick inside the Molly Brown (who had weathered the fallout from the corned beef sandwich scandal), would attempt to make sure that they did while taking his first shot at command. Chosen to accompany him on the journey was a most extraordinary gentleman.

# CHAPTER 7

# Enter the Renaissance Man

**M**ike Collins had "slept like a baby" until almost noon on July 18, 1966. This, however, was not another case of an astronaut trying to beat a hangover after having had a wild night at the Cape. For one of the few times in NASA history, the flight plan for Gemini X called for a late afternoon launch and Deke had encouraged Mike and his commander, Gemini 3 veteran John W. Young, to sleep in as long as possible on the morning of the scheduled launch. Who knew? Maybe NASA might actually get both the Agena target vehicle and Gemini X off their pads and into orbit today. In the hours to come, both astronauts would be thankful for the extra time in the sack because the mission upon which they were about to embark was to be the most complex and ambitious yet attempted in the brief history of human spaceflight.

Michael "Mike" Collins was born in Rome, Italy on Halloween in 1930, the only son of James Lawton Collins, a career Army officer who would retire as a major (two star) general. His father's younger brother, General Joseph "Lightning Joe" Lawton Collins, served in both the European and Pacific theaters in World War II and would serve as chief of staff of the United States Army throughout the entire duration of the Korean War. As the result of his being born into the family of a high-ranking career military officer, young Michael would have an upbringing that was far more cosmopolitan and diverse than his colleagues in the astronaut corps who for the most part were from the Midwest or were farmboys or were both. Before the age of 17, Mike had lived in Italy, Puerto

Rico, New York, San Antonio and Alexandria, Virginia. After the outbreak of World War II, the family settled in Washington D.C. where Mike graduated from St. Alban's School in 1948.

Considering that he'd grown up surrounded by more brass than Herb Alpert, young Michael had admirably resisted the temptation to become the embodiment of the term "Army brat." Still, while he refused to flaunt his impressive military lineage, he had the good sense not to rebel against it either. Eventually, he decided to join the family business and was admitted to West Point where he graduated with the Class of 1952. It was at that stage of his life that he decided to take something of a detour. Because his uncle was at that moment the highest ranking officer in the regular Army and fearing that any advancement—particularly rapid advancement—that he might make through that branch of the service could be attributed to nepotism, Mike chose to further his military career in the United States Air Force. His service would both require and enable him to relive the nomadic nature of his childhood and he would eventually be stationed in France where he would meet his future wife, Patricia Finnegan.

Along the journey, he would cultivate an appreciation for gourmet food and fine wine which would stand in stark contrast to the whiskey, beer and barbeque crowd at Edwards. Not that Mike felt any particular compulsion to fit in or be pigeonholed. His decision to go into the Air Force was proof enough of that. Later in life, he would even go so far as to describe some of the military leaders he'd served with as "lemming-like" for what he perceived to be their inability and/or unwillingness to engage in creative thinking or to stray too far off the intellectual beaten path. Still, Mike himself would not be able to wander too far astray if he wanted to advance his flying career and, like so many of his NASA colleagues, he would attend the Experimental Test Pilot School at Edwards. Despite the rigidity of the indoctrination into that elite fraternity, Collins would always remain far more renaissance man than fighter jock or, as Norman Mailer would succinctly put it some years later, "Collins was cool."

On October 14, 1963, Mike got the call from Deke and the cool one joined NASA as an astronaut with the rest of Group 3. After backing up Gemini VII with John Young, per Deke's standard rotation the pair would go prime on Gemini X. The combination of the ultra-smooth Collins with the laconic all-business Young meant that this crew was not apt to be one of the more talkative that NASA had thus far sent up. Because the guys in Mission Control were operating on a need–to–know–right–goddamned–now basis with regard to flight crew operations and because John and Mike tended to not be chatty, it was inevitable that some friction would arise between the crew and the ground during the flight and that some allowances would end up having to be made on both sides.

One topic about which Commander Young had no difficulty speaking out was the Gemini X flight plan. When he'd initially heard the announced mission objectives, the first words out of his mouth were, "They must be out of their minds." It was not an irrational observation. First would come the Agena launch. Then, if it didn't explode (like it already had—twice) Gemini X would blast into orbit and attempt to rendezvous with it. While in pursuit, Collins would do a stand-up EVA requiring a cockpit depressurization/repressurization during which he'd try to employ navigational techniques using star sightings. After getting Mike back inside, Gemini X would complete the rendezvous with Agena 10 and dock with it and if the conjoined spacecraft didn't start tumbling like a barrel going over Niagara Falls (like it already had—during Gemini VIII) then Young would undock and redock a few times. "Practicing" docking they called it because only doing it once without damaging either vehicle or endangering the crew apparently wasn't enough. Then, they'd fly up to 475 miles on the Agena's engine to set a new altitude record, stay aloft for several hours, burn their way back down a couple hundred miles and undock a final time from Agena 10. Assuming they were still alive at that point, they would go and rendezvous with Gemini VIII's Agena which was still up there orbiting the Earth because … it was still up there one would guess but who the hell really knew? Then, once the rendezvous with Agena 8 was completed, Collins would go outside the spacecraft on a second EVA, float over to Agena 8 and retrieve an experimental micrometeorite package from the exterior of the vehicle, replace it with a new one (ostensibly for some other unlucky neophyte to come back and retrieve on a later mission) after which Collins would space-walk back to Young, climb back inside and the two would back away from Agena 8. After that, they'd do a third depressurization/repressurization to dump Mike's EVA umbilical and all their other trash and, finally, they'd orbit for another day, fire their retros and then splash down within sight of the recovery ship. When one took all that into account, perhaps John was right. Maybe they had lost their cotton-picking minds.

As it turned out, July 18th would be the day when John's theory regarding the collective mental health of NASA management would begin to be put to the test. Of course, before the trip out to Pad 19 could be undertaken, the traditional pre-flight rituals had to be carefully observed. During the suiting up process, Collins recalled having to hook himself up to a receptacle in the corner of his urine collection bag. These condom-like devices had been sized by NASA as small, medium and large. When the astronauts got word of NASA's measuremental terminology, they immediately insisted that the sizings be upgraded to extra-large, immense and unbelievable. Apparently, these guys had egos that were even larger than unbelievable. Once securely mated to their urine bags and fully denitrogenated, it was off to the gantry. In the weeks preceding the launch, Young had expressed concern that the lack of flexibility in his spacesuit gloves might cause him to have difficulty with some of the onboard activities which would task the dexterity of his hands and fingers. Accordingly, he had requested that he be allowed to bring a pair of pliers along with him. When NASA predictably refused, John snuck them onboard anyway. After smuggling a corned beef sandwich aboard Gemini 3, he probably figured he could get a hedge trimmer past them if he really needed to.

Once safely strapped down inside the spacecraft atop GT-X, the crew breathed "a sigh of relief" upon being informed that the Agena had arrived safely in orbit. Now it was their turn. As Kraft, Hodge and Kranz had all now moved on to the Apollo program, Glynn Lunney would take the reins as prime flight director in Mission Control and he anxiously awaited his first launch in the big chair. Precisely on schedule at 5:20 p.m. local time, the Titan roared to life. At just about four and a half minutes in, with Collins marveling at the view, Young chided him to "Put your head back in the cockpit," an admonition which he would feel compelled to repeat to his rookie pilot on several occasions during the first orbit. Lunney had the Capcom radio up that they looked good for a fourth orbit rendezvous with Agena 10.

Before they began positioning themselves for that, Collins immediate task was to haul out a Kollsman sextant and attempt some onboard star sightings through the Gemini's tiny window. The purpose of the exercise was to see if the crew could rendezvous with a target in space—in this case Agena 10—by using only onboard navigation with no assistance from the ground. Collins had difficulty from the outset. The primary problem was that Mike had a rough time distinguishing the horizon from a band of radiant light in the upper atmosphere called the "airglow." Trying to keep his buddy's head up, Young barked "What the heck! If you can't see the stars, you can't see them..." when Collins groaned that he was doing "a lousy job." With a flight plan this jampacked, there was no time for any such regrets. It was time to start honing in on the rendezvous with Agena 10 which would now have to be conducted using the ground's computer.

Unfortunately, Young's approach to the target vehicle did not go much better than Mike's attempt at onboard navigation. While aligning the platform for the final maneuver up to the Agena ("terminal phase adjustment" Mission Control called it) John didn't realize that the spacecraft had turned slightly. As a result, they got to within 600 feet of the Agena when they effectively hit a wall in space. At 5:13:14, Young could be heard calling out "Whoa, whoa, whoa, you bum!" Intuitively, both crewmen knew what had to be done. John would have to fly a corkscrew maneuver that the astronauts called a "whifferdil" which would spiral them toward the Agena. At 5:21:31, Capcom called up with a somewhat meek "You there yet?" which Young rogered. A half hour later Young was able to report that docking had been achieved and that the vehicles were "rigid," a NASA-esque way of letting Lunney and his troops know that they weren't tumbling out of control like Gemini VIII.

At 6:01:17, Hawaii Capcom rather unhelpfully informed them that they'd used a "tremendous amount" of fuel during the whifferdil. "Goddammit, we know that," Collins thought, "The question is where to go from here." Mike's immediate concern was that the excessive fuel consumption might compromise his scheduled EVA activities or cause them to be canceled altogether. Fortunately, that would not be necessary. However, the crew did have to scrub the "practice docking" which would have involved pulling back and redocking with the Agena due to the mission's new fuel constraints.

Now, it was on to uncharted territory. One of the perks of the LOR mode of going to the moon aboard two separate independently functioning spacecraft was that there would be added redundancy in the propulsion department in the event that one of the main engines on either spacecraft became inoperative. With Gemini X now safely docked with the target vehicle in a stable configuration, the next task—and a primary mission objective—was to fire the Agena's engine and have it lift the conjoined vehicles to a record orbital altitude of approximately 475 miles.

Since Gemini X and Agena 10 were docked nose-to-nose with the astronauts looking at the target vehicle, the Agena's rocket was pointed away from them. That meant that when the Agena's rocket was engaged, the two astronauts would experience thrust to the front of their bodies, like a stomach punch, which would result in an "eyeballs-out" sensation which is the exact opposite of every rocket firing from beneath every previous crew which had been accomplished up to that point. At ignition, Young was subdued and noted, "It's pretty damn hard to talk" when flying backward at negative one G. For 80 seconds, the Agena's engine (which Collins described as "raucous") elevated them higher than any human being had ever flown before. The ride was so intense that after shutdown, Collins told Young at 7:44:37 that he'd "almost shut it down." When Young scoffed, Collins insisted, saying, "If you had said shit, I would have shut it down. Really." Young replied that it was a good thing that he'd been "too busy hanging on the wall" to say anything to provoke Collins. So there they were hanging in space 475 miles up. That would be enough exertion for the spacecraft, Agena 10 and the crew for day one and at 9:03:59 John and Mike signed off for the night.

The high point of the first rest period came when the guys unpacked the plates to cover their windows during the rest period. On the inside of each plate, some generous soul had pasted a picture of a scantily-clad extremely well-proportioned young lady. Whether it was the images of the girls or the strange environment or a combination of the two, Collins had a horrible time getting to sleep. As he began to doze, Mike became so concerned that his floating hands might accidentally hit a switch and trigger a crisis that he actually considered stuffing them into his mouth.

With precious little rest, the crew was ready to push on with the day two flight plan. The first major maneuver was to be an Agena burn which would serve both to circularize and lower their orbit thereby beginning their pursuit of Agena 8. Once completed, it was then time for Mike to perform his first EVA. At 23:22:37, Mike reported that cabin depressurization had begun. Perhaps because of Cernan's ordeal, NASA was only going to allow Mike to dip his toe into the pool during this first "stand-up EVA." Essentially, this exercise would have Mike on the umbilical at which time he would stand up on his seat and perform a series of tasks consisting primarily of photography.

Before they were able to get everything squared away and pop open the hatch, came an unwelcome kick in the pants from Slayton. At 23:05:28, the call came up, "John this is Deke." Oh shit. Under normal flight conditions, the Capcom—and only the Capcom—is allowed to communicate with the crew in flight. It was one of Kraft's golden rules of flight control and it was imposed to eliminate chatter and crosstalk from the ground which could distract and/or confuse the crew. Accordingly, when Slayton cut into the loop, John and Mike each grabbed their balls. Here it came. "You guys are doing a commendable job of maintaining radio silence... why don't you guys do a little more talking from here on?" Ouch. Young, already smarting from the previous day's excessive fuel consumption and in no mood to be jerked around snapped back, "Okay, what do you want us to talk about?" Collins, sensing that things were rapidly heading south, started "singing like a canary" just to initiate some dialogue with the ground. When the Capcom later piped up the score of that day's Mets-Astros game, Collins thought, "Jesus Christ! Here I am asshole-deep in a 131 step EVA checklist and they want to talk about baseball." Still, tolerating such useless banter was way better than having a pissed-off Deke Slayton.

Thankfully, they finally got the pressure dumped sufficiently for Collins to throw open the hatch and begin the stand-up EVA. Before Mike could finish his assigned tasks, he began to experience a burning sensation in both eyes which caused them to tear up. Young, understandably not wanting to mess with Collins' EVA, then felt free to admit that he was having the same problem. As there was no way for either man to clear his eyes, the EVA had to be terminated immediately six minutes ahead of schedule. This was by no means a mission critical occurrence but with a far more ambitious outside–the-spacecraft EVA still to come, it was a problem that Mission Control had to set about solving immediately. Fortunately, they pegged the problem as both astronauts having their suits fans on simultaneously. When Mike went out next time, John's suit fan would stay off. When Collins got back inside, for the first time in the program the crew had no difficulty getting the hatch to close and lock. After repressurization, it was time to put a bow on day two. Fortunately, the crew slept much more soundly during their second attempt and their eye irritation soon showed substantial improvement.

The flight plan for the third day of Gemini X would entail some of the greatest challenges of the entire mission. In order, the crew would have to get off and get away from Agena 10 and then rendezvous with Agena 8. Then, Mike would do an EVA over to Agena 8 and secure a micrometeorite package from the exterior of the vehicle which Dave Scott was to have retrieved had the Gemini VIII mission not been aborted. The first step in that process called for Gemini X to use Agena 10's engine for one last burn to close the gap with Agena 8. The crew had been riding Agena 10 for 39 hours now which was 22 hours longer than the flight plan had them scheduled to be docked. As it turned out, having Agena 10's fuel supply had been, as Collins had termed it, a "godsend," due to the crew's ability to use Agena 10's fuel supply to cover the shortage in Gemini X caused by the excessive usage during the whifferdilled rendezvous. Once the burn was finished, Gemini X was finally able to undock from Agena 10. At that moment, Gemini X was 132 miles away from Agena 8 and eight miles below it. At 46:15:44 Gemini X's fuel cut-off for the upcoming rendezvous was pegged by Mission Control at 7%. Young got them there with 15% remaining. Now it was Mike's turn.

At dawn, Mission Control gave a go for the EVA. With a reply that could not have warmed Slayton's heart, Young copied with a "Glad you said that. Mike's going outside right now." Collins' first task on emerging from the spacecraft was to hook up his zip gun to a nitrogen line on the exterior of the ship. Thus would begin a perilous ballet between Young inside Gemini X, Agena 8 and Collins on the outside. With Mike now out of the hatch, this would be the first time in the history of spaceflight that a commander was going to be required to hold station with a separate unmanned vehicle while simultaneously having a crewmate outside. Mike's primary problem was his proximity to the ship, particularly OAMS thruster # 16, which if fired by Young at an inopportune moment could do all kinds of damage to Mike and/ or his spacesuit. John's primary problem was that he had to make use of the OAMS capability—perhaps including thruster # 16—if he was going to keep Gemini X from smacking into Agena 8. As a result, there was an ongoing dialogue with Mike imploring John not to scorch him and Young reminding him essentially, "Yeah

Mike, I hear you but I really need not to bump into this son-of-a-bitch. So, you're gonna have to watch your own back out there while I make sure not to crash this ship that's gotta take us home tomorrow." Obviously, it was a delicate balancing act for each of them.

Despite experiencing some Cernanesque problems with the nitrogen line, Mike was ready to get moving before something truly bad could happen. At 48:55:41 he gave an "I'm going to leap for her" and pushed himself toward Agena 8. To his immense relief, he was straight-lining toward Agena 8's docking cone close to where the micrometeorite package was located and was able to grab the smooth lip of the cone. Since there were no handholds on the Agena (I mean, why make it easy?), Collins tried to hand-over-hand it around the cone to the pack when he encountered a discharge ring on the cone which looked like "a scythe with a wicked hook" two feet in diameter. While simultaneously trying to avoid it and reach for the pack, Mike lost his grip and began to cartwheel away from the Agena like one of the Flying fucking Wallendas. After a disorienting moment or two, he gathered himself sufficiently to grab the zip gun on his hip and maneuver himself back behind Gemini X where he would reinitiate his death dance with thruster # 16. Fortunately, he made it back to the hatch without getting fried or wrapping his umbilical around the ship. Once there, he grabbed on and decided to make another run at Agena 8 using the zip gun. Only this time, he closed in on it too fast and had to drop the gun and reach out for the Agena. Ramming his right hand into a recessed area behind the docking collar, Mike was able to grab a handful of loose wires to secure himself. He then reached around and ripped off the pack and then—somehow—got back to Gemini X without tearing his suit on the scythe-hook or tangling himself in the tether. The flight plan had called for Mike to slap a new pack on Agena 8. When John asked Mike if he'd gotten the new pack on, Mike replied, "No, and I'm not going to." Fair enough. When Mission Control advised that Gemini X's fuel situation was becoming borderline critical, John said, "Well, then, he'd better get back in." With that, he instructed Mike to "get out of all that garbage" and "come back in the house." Unlike Ed White, Collins did not protest his commander's order to reenter the spacecraft in the least.

Once they'd gotten the hatch closed—thankfully, for the first time in program history they'd gotten through a mission without that exercise causing any palpitations in Mission Control—the crew was able to turn their attention to more mundane chores. After a third and final three minute "EVA" to dump Mike's umbilical and the rest of their trash, one final burn would reduce their altitude and put them in position for retrofire. After a rest period, Canary Capcom rousted the crew at 62:45:37 and had them begin their final day preparation. Seven hours later, they were on the NASA victory lap thanking all of the tracking station personnel along the way. Over California and approaching Houston, John asked Ed White if "super-retro" was down in Mission Control to pull their fat out of the fire if anything went sideways. "Super-retro" was none other than John Llewellyn and he was on console. An hour later, Collins confirmed that all four retros had fired and that they were on their way down. At 70:43:43, Houston Capcom advised, "You're on television" meaning that the recovery forces aboard the Guadalcanal had a visual on them. Three minutes later, they were safely on the water with the ship upright and the chutes laying alongside. Gemini X was home.

Out of the water but not yet out of the woods, it would turn out, as John and Mike still had to endure the post-flight debriefing and press conference—and damned if a problem hadn't arisen. Remember the two Miss January-types from the window shade plates? As it turned out, they were bunnies at the St. Louis Playboy Club who were friends with the McDonnell engineer who was in charge of packing the window shades. When the engineer told the girls about what he'd done with those pictures he'd taken of them awhile back, the lovelies vowed to show up at the post-flight press conference to claim their hard-earned fifteen minutes of fame. Then word of the situation got out at McDonnell and eventually made its way back to Slayton. Just knowing that the bunnies would fire off a giggly-jiggly "What was it like going around the world with us, boys?"—type question, Deke threatened the McDonnell engineer with everything short of death by slow torture if the girls popped up at an inopportune moment at the NASA auditorium. Fortunately for everyone involved, they stayed in St. Louis.

WITH THE BUNNY CRISIS averted, there was the usual self-analysis to be done. Particularly when viewed against the backdrop of NASA's two previous missions, Gemini X was nothing less than a spectacular success. Rendezvous, a bold wager upon which NASA had pushed its entire stack of chips into the center of the table without even knowing if it could be done, had now become almost routine. Just as importantly, the docking gremlins of Gemini VIII had been banished forever with the brilliant work of Young and Collins while attached to Agena 10. Added to that was the flawless maneuvering of the conjoined vehicles using the propulsion systems of each one. Geminis V and VII had each already proven that durability of spacecraft or crew wasn't going to be a show-stopper. But that still left EVA. Collins and White had both fared far better than Cernan almost by default (apologies Geno) primarily because they'd had the zip gun to stop them from tumbling after they'd lost control of their center of mass. Still, Collins had hardly had an easy time of it. His treks over to Agena 8 could only generously be described as spacewalks. In truth, the whole endeavor had many of the earmarks of a stunt more worthy of Evel Knievel than of a scientific undertaking worthy of an astronaut. As out of control as he was out there at times, Mike could have smashed visor-first into Gemini X or Agena 8. Also, there had been the appendages with sharp edges protruding from Agena 8 that could have sliced Mike's suit to bits. Either of those things could have easily killed him and the skill he demonstrated in avoiding them had been commendable. Still, there was no doubt that Mike had been extremely lucky out there as well. Despite Mike's best efforts, it could not be denied that—with just two remaining flights scheduled in the program—EVA was still the primary monkey in

NASA's wrench. There simply had to be a better way to accomplish this crucial task that had thus far frustratingly remained just beyond their ability to grasp. An all-Navy crew on Gemini XI would get the next crack at slaying the extravehicular dragon.

# CHAPTER 8

# 850 Down; 239,150 to Go

**W**ith the ink blots, enema bags and the rest of NASA's flight surgeon horseshit now completely in his rearview mirror, it was time for Pete Conrad to take a well-earned stab at command. Deke was happy to give him that shot on Gemini XI. As well advertised as Pete's love of the Navy was, no Air Force pilot in the world had a shot at the right hand seat on this mission. The only question was which naval aviator would be going up with Pete. There wasn't a great deal of suspense about who that guy would be either.

Richard F. "Dick" Gordon, Jr. was born October 5, 1929 in Seattle. He graduated from the University of Washington with a B.S. in chemistry in 1951. Upon leaving college, Dick joined the Navy and earned his aviator's wings in 1953. After attending all weather flight school and jet transitional training, he was assigned to an all weather fighter squadron stationed in Jacksonville. On a tour of duty aboard the carrier USS Ranger, he had bunked in the same quarters as a certain Charles Conrad, Jr. and the two had become close friends. In 1957, Dick shipped out to Pax River and served as a test pilot. During the hitch, one of his flight instructors had been Al Shepard. After flying a number of the Navy's hottest planes, Dick became the first project test pilot for the F4H Phantom II and participated in the introduction of that aircraft into both the Atlantic and Pacific fleets. Then, in May, 1961, he won the prestigious Bendix Trophy while setting a Los Angeles to New York transcontinental speed record of 2 hours and 47 minutes. Extremely well–connected in military circles, Dick knew half of the Mercury astronauts on a first name basis before he ever even applied to NASA.

Gordon certainly appeared to be a prime candidate, if not a shoo-in, for selection as a Group 2 astronaut. When he found out that he hadn't made it, Dick was not merely disappointed that he hadn't made the grade. The sting of the rejection coupled with the fact that his old pal Pete Conrad had been picked had served to really (like REALLY) piss him off. So much so that Dick not only scratched NASA off his list of potential future employers but he also actually considered resigning his Navy commission as well. Sympathizing with his friend's frustration and recognizing the fact that he was letting his anger cloud his judgment, Pete decided to intervene. In a barroom pep talk that was equal parts pat on the shoulder and kick in the ass, Conrad pointed out to his pal that NASA wasn't going to get to the moon with only sixteen astronauts. There would be other slots available down the line if Dick just kept his head on straight and his hat in the ring. "And why would I do that?" Gordon groused as they knocked back another round. With his trademark gap-toothed grin, Pete replied, "Because you miss me." So, whether it was Pete's persuasive charm, Dick yielding to the logic of the situation or whether it was simply a matter of them both being so loaded that any idea sounded like a good idea, Dick took his buddy's advice. As usual, it was right on the money and Gordon was selected to join NASA with Group 3 in October, 1963.

Down through the years, Conrad had taken to calling Gordon "Dickie—Dickie" and "The Animal." Why "The Animal" you ask? Dick Gordon was the kind of guy, well, how does one say it? Imagine that there was a hypothetical NASA housewife who'd had a highball or three too many at a company barbeque and decided—hypothetically, of course—to cast a furtive glance at the hindquarters of one of her husband's colleagues. Under those circumstances, it was a pretty good bet that the backside being ogled was attached to Dick Gordon. Not that Dick did anything in particular to encourage it. He was the kind of guy that, as they said in the '60s, chicks just dug.

As to the pairing with Conrad, Slayton didn't exactly have to be a soothsayer to sign off on this one. These two guys were so tight it would have been a mistake not to pair them up. Heaven knows neither Pete or Dick would have had it any other way and it was a decision Deke would never have the slightest reason to regret. The pair became "virtually inseparable" as Guenter Wendt described them and over time the two would develop the ability to communicate with one another through facial expressions and body language without either ever having to speak. Gemini XI would be their very own all–Navy showcase.

As with every previous mission, Gemini XI had a fully–loaded flight plan. While the primary program objectives had in a technical sense already been achieved, that didn't mean that there wasn't still some new ground for the crew to break. As to rendezvous, previous crews had proven that it could be accomplished as early as the third orbit after launch. That was fine for proving that the theory could be taken to the application stage and then to refine the maneuver. But because of the weight and, hence, fuel constraints of both the CSM and LM spacecrafts on a lunar landing mission, the pilots of those vehicles weren't going to have the luxury of being able to drift aimlessly around the moon hoping they'd eventually find one another. To the contrary, because of the limited amounts of fuel involved, rendezvous after coming up off of the surface of the moon would have to be achieved in one orbit. M = 1. Gemini XI would be the first mission to attempt it.

As to docking, NASA truly wanted to see whether the pilots and hardware could dock multiple times during a flight. Even on an emergency–free lunar voyage, the CSM and LM would still have to dock twice. First while moving away from Earth when the CSM would have to fly free then turn around and pluck the LM out of the top of the Saturn V's third stage while in transit to the moon and then again around the moon prior to coming home. Of course, NASA had wanted to do multiple docking maneuvers on Gemini X but Young's whifferdil on the approach to Agena 10 had precluded that. So Pete and Dick would try it again.

Then, of course, there was EVA. NASA was still grappling with the perception that astronauts might not be able to do useful work in the weightless environment of space. That the perception still existed at this stage of the program was less than ideal considering that Congress ultimately controlled NASA's budget. Accordingly, NASA really needed to start demonstrating that it could do pretty much whatever it wanted to do in space whenever it wanted to do it in order to ensure that the federal funding spigot would not be turned off. If Gordon could manage to execute a steady, problem-free EVA, it would undoubtedly help alleviate that concern.

Having heard some rumblings about the Russians possibly planning some sort of manned lunar flyaround, NASA naturally responded with some talk about sending a Gemini spacecraft on a long loop around the moon just to make sure that the Soviet Union didn't do it first. If they did, the Russians would undoubtedly claim that circumnavigation was all they ever intended to do from the outset and declare victory in the space race. Pete, of course, was totally gung–ho. Alas, the rumblings turned out to be only that so NASA dialed everything back. Still, Pete very much wanted to set a new altitude record. His problem was that NASA wasn't going to let him go up and do it just to go up and do it. That meant that the agency was going to require some sort of reason to sign off on the maneuver. So Pete came up with one. At that time, satellites were already flying higher up than Gemini X had gone and were sending back black and white photographs of the Earth taken from that altitude. So, Pete decided to sell NASA on the idea that he'd fly Gemini XI up that high and take color pictures of the planet so that the two could be compared. It was a half–assed idea but it was better than nothing and since nearly everybody upstairs was pretty much crazy about Pete, NASA decided it was good enough and approved Pete's request to take Gemini XI and the Agena up to an altitude of 850 miles.

For the last major objective of the flight, Gordon was to attach a 100 foot tether between the Gemini and the Agena during his initial EVA. Later, during the last day of the flight, Pete was to undock the vehicles and then try to stretch the tether between the two until it was fully extended. Then, he would attempt to get the two spinning around the tether like some crazy ride at a county fair. NASA's stated purpose for doing this was to see if this motion would create positive gravity in the weightless environment. This, of course, would have absolutely no practical application in either the Gemini or Apollo programs. At best, it might provide data with which some sort of 2001–esque ever-spinning ferris–wheel–type device could be built on a space station or a manned mission to Mars *way* on down the line. Why NASA would even think about doing something like this now was baffling to put it in the most generous possible terms.

After two previous scrubs, Pete and Dick were hoping that the third time would be a charm for Gemini XI on September 12, 1966. At 8:05 a.m. the Atlas/Agena was launched from Pad 14. Because of the M=1 mission objective, XI would have just a two *second* launch window to have a chance at successfully completing the task and at 9:42:26:5, they hit it. The liftoff was greeted by a boisterous "Go, you big mother!" from the mission commander. At 5:58 the Capcom gave the crew the "Go" for first orbit rendezvous. From that point, the crew was out of communications range during much of the requisite maneuvering. Finally, over Hawaii at 1:16:16, Conrad called that they had the Agena at 15,000 feet. In fact, once they'd attained orbital insertion and turned on the rendezvous radar, they got a ping from the Agena immediately. Three minutes later, Pete began braking and at 1:25:13 advised "We're here." They'd done it. Rendezvous after just a single orbit. A jubilant Dick Gordon had a message for the man many of the astronauts reverently referred to as "Flight." At 1:30:15, Dick radioed, "Tell Mr. Kraft—would he believe M equals 1."

Three minutes later they were given a go for docking and moments later Pete advised that the maneuver had successfully been accomplished. About a half hour after that, Conrad called to report that they'd undocked and they proceeded with the practice docking exercise which Gemini X had been unable to undertake. During the maneuver, Pete handed control of the vehicle over to Gordon. At 3:19:20, the call came "Mark one docking for Richard

Gordon." While it had been uncommon for a pilot to take control of the spacecraft during a Gemini mission, NASA wanted
as many astronauts as possible to gain experience with docking
maneuvers. Gordon later joked he'd have thrown Pete "out of the
spacecraft" if Pete hadn't let him have a go at it. A few hours later,
Dick successfully accomplished it again. At 7:46:26, Conrad powered down the UHF and bid the ground good night. Day one had
been an unmitigated success.

Day two, as Chris Kraft would later reminisce, was when
"things went to hell." The primary mission objective that day was
Gordon's EVA outside the spacecraft. Unfortunately, the guys had
problems almost from the beginning. At 20:11:08, Dick advised
they were beginning their EVA prep checklist. Per the flight plan,
hatch opening was still four hours away. Pete and Dick, always
eager for action, blew through the checklist in a little under an
hour. That, in turn, would have them fully suited and awaiting
the start of the EVA inside the cockpit for the next three hours.
Gordon's use of his suit's umbilical and heat exchanger systems—
which were designed for use in space and not meant to be used
in the climate-controlled cockpit—caused him to overheat. So
they had to switch him back to the ship's system. Then, still fully
suited, Dick had a hell of a time getting his sun visor attached to
his helmet which further taxed him physically and caused him
to start getting overheated again. Finally, Dick announced hatch
opening at 24:02:07. Just six minutes later, barely into his scheduled 115 minute spacewalk, Dick was already gassed. "Got to rest
here a minute" he said. One of his primary objectives on the EVA
was to attach the tether between the two vehicles for the artificial
gravity experiment to be conducted later in the flight. Dick got
it done by wrapping his legs around the Gemini's nose but he
was using the large muscles in his legs continually just to hold on.
"Ride 'em cowboy!" Pete encouraged, and to Dick's credit, he got
the tether attached. The next exchange between the two, however,
pretty much told the story. At 24:10:30 Pete asked, "How are you
doing?" to which Dick responded simply, "Tired, Pete." Conrad

then encouraged Dick to "Just rest" followed by an almost plaintive "You've only been out nine minutes."

By the time Dick got the tether attached, sweat had begun pouring into his right eye both stinging and blinding him. At that point, for one of the few times in his career, Pete Conrad felt fear. Yeah, Pete had had the same pre-flight EVA chat with Slayton that Stafford and Young did. The difference was that if either of those guys was confronted with the unthinkable they were going to be faced with having to jettison a fellow astronaut and colleague. For Pete, it would be like cutting his brother loose out there and then having to wave goodbye to him through that tiny little window. Then having to close the hatch and come down alone. Then having to live with that memory for the rest of his life. Anyone who'd known Pete Conrad for longer than five minutes knew there was no way in hell he'd *ever* do that to Dick Gordon. No way he'd ever allow the situation to deteriorate to the point that he might even have to consider it. As a result, it was a damned short leash that Dickie–Dickie was on out there. By 24:40:33, the jig was up and Pete called down, "Listen, I just brought Dick back in." After explaining to the ground why the scheduled hour and 45 minute EVA had to be aborted after only 35 minutes, Conrad called it a wrap on day two at 31:33:51.

At just a little under thirty nine hours, the crew began day three transmissions. It was time for Pete and Dick to go set a new altitude record. During their 26th orbit, Pete sent the command to fire the Agena's engine for a 26 second burst that would take the crew higher than any human had ever gone before. At 41:02:40, after successfully completing the climb, Conrad confirmed the suspicions of many when he advised, "It's go up here and the world's round." They had topped out at 850 miles. Only 239,150 more to go and John Kennedy's goal could be fulfilled. Still, for the moment anyway, this perch suited Pete and Dick just fine. "You can't believe it," said Pete, "the curvature of the Earth stands out a lot." And, as promised, the guys took their color pictures.

Alas, their view from the top of the world didn't last long and after an Agena burn down to a lower orbit, it was time for Dick to have another go at EVA. This time it would be of the much less risky "stand–up" variety. It would turn out to be far less eventful than the previous day's misadventure and that in itself was a blessing. In fact, it was so tranquil that during a night pass, Conrad piped up and said, "Hey Dick, you'll never believe it ... I fell asleep" to which Gordon replied, "Huh ... what?" Dick had fallen asleep as well. At 47:34:05, Gordon advised Mission Control, "You've got two guys taking catnaps up here." Forty five minutes later, they'd finished with their photography assignment and sealed the hatch.

Closing in on fifty hours into the mission, the crew separated from the Agena. Now it was time for the great tether experiment. With the benefit of hindsight, it's hard to comprehend why NASA would even dream of doing it. Great care had always been taken during rendezvous and docking maneuvers to keep the two vehicles from colliding with one another. Hell, Armstrong and Scott had almost bought the farm when the two went into a tumble while they were attached. Now NASA was going to risk one or both of them going into a tumble while they were undocked and within mere feet of each other.

Pete hammered home the point early in the exercise when he advised that he'd "hit" and "really upset" the Agena. Not good. Then came calls from Pete that the tether was "whipping around us" and making "a looping motion" between the two spacecraft like a huge jump rope. Really? Minutes later, Pete followed that up with a "This is not going to work." Gordon then expressed reservations about going into a night pass hooked together like they were. They pressed on but when Mission Control asked them to increase their spin rate, Pete fired back, "What'll it prove?"

Eventually they did in fact create a very minimal amount of artificial gravity as demonstrated by the fact that objects inside the ship were floating in a straight line toward the tether but they were wasting fuel. Without enough gas, they would not be able to get unwound if this damn thing wrapped around them and then Pete reported, "We've got oscillations everywhere." Finally, at 52:50:36, they blew the docking bar and cut the tether loose. Afterward, the tether immediately started to wrap around the Agena. So Pete got the hell away from it. After a couple more hours of picture taking, the guys were ready to put a bow on day three, signing off at 58:09:59.

Nearly seven hours later, the crew powered up and aligned the platform. In a few hours, they would be coming home. Before they did, since they still had some fuel in the tank, NASA wanted them to rendezvous one last time with the Agena. To some, it may have seemed like overkill but to NASA any kind of rendezvous was a good method for obtaining data that might be of use in any type of emergency that might crop up on a future mission. Pete and Dick closed from 24 miles to 50 feet when Gordon advised "That's the best I can give you."

At 67:48:49, Conrad advised that the flight plan was complete, their gear was stowed and they were ready to come down. Two hours later, the crew started the victory lap with a thank you to Canary Capcom. The reentry was to be the first fully controlled automatically by the ship's computer. Retrofire began at 70:41:37. A half hour later, recovery forces aboard the USS Guam advised that they had a visual of the ship. It was September 15, 1966 and Gemini XI was home.

WHEN THE TIME CAME for Pete and Dick to sign their score-cards, they had checked every box for Gemini XI. Except one. The outside–the–spacecraft EVA had once again gone horribly wrong. Suiting up, doing the cabin depress, popping the hatch, standing up in the seat and getting back inside had all been accomplished with an acceptable degree of success. That wasn't small potatoes given that verifying the integrity of the suits and the operational capability of the hatches, latches and other hardware in the vacuum of space were all significant hurdles which NASA had to clear in order to push ahead. Still, it could not be denied that when guys had gotten their feet outside the spacecraft, EVA had been a completely different ballgame. Adding to the problem was the fact that the flight schedule had become so compressed due to the impending start of the Apollo program that future EVA astronauts were not really being given time to analyze the data from previous spacewalks or even to discuss the problems in any significant detail with their colleagues who had made them. As a result, the EVA astronauts kept making the same mistakes over and over again with the same consequences—specifically overheating, fogging up and sweating into the eyes to the point of causing incapacity. At the heart of it all was the excessive fatigue caused by the wrestling match that each EVA astronaut had had with himself just trying to keep his body stable relative to the spacecraft or the Agena. Moreover, it was a two–pronged failure—one of both the technique being employed and the equipment being used to carry out the appointed tasks. Gemini only had one last crack at getting EVA right before the clock ran out on the program. It was going to take some nuanced and innovative thinking if NASA was to accomplish this last unfulfilled Gemini objective during the final flight of the program.

# CHAPTER 9

# Bringing Down the Curtain

After the success of Gemini VII, Jim Lovell was the NASA equivalent of a made man. Almost as good was the fact that he stood in well with Frank Borman, the Group 2 golden boy who had been just the second member of that class to command a Gemini mission. Since Deke had waved Borman on through to Apollo, Frank was damn near bound to secure the command of one of the prime missions of the program. It wasn't a flight of fancy for Lovell to imagine that Frank might just want to take him along for the ride. Better still, the two rookies had taken on the ultimate Gemini turdhunt—the two week duration flight—without flinching and had not only survived the ordeal but had actually flourished during their two weeks in the men's room. Surely all that had to count for something. Now if he could just keep from going blind—or contracting Meniere's disease—the future looked awfully promising for James Arthur Lovell.

At the beginning of 1966, things didn't look quite so rosy for Buzz Aldrin. Deke had already handed out the command assignments for Geminis IX through XI and with Stafford and Cernan backing up See and Bassett on IX, Tom and Gene were probably a lock to go prime on Gemini XII, the last scheduled flight of the program. Hell, Deke was already planning to stick Elliot into the dreaded spot of backup commander for Gemini XII which would ice him deep into the Apollo program and well past the first lunar landing missions if he ever flew again at all. As gloomy as the outlook was for Elliot See, it was still better than where Aldrin stood at that point. At least Elliot was going to fly a Gemini mission. Buzz, slotted as the pilot on the backup crew for Gemini X, stood to come out of the program with no spaceflight experience whatsoever. That all changed on February 28, 1966. The tragic deaths of See and Bassett meant that the flight rotation music started playing again and when it stopped this time, Buzz would no longer be standing up. After the funerals, Deke moved Stafford and Cernan up to prime on IX and then named Lovell and Aldrin to back them up. That meant that if Buzz could just find a way to get along with Lovell, perhaps the most affable guy in the astronaut corps, and manage not to screw the pooch during training then he might well find himself on the prime crew of Gemini XII. If that one broke Buzz's way, that would put him in the hunt for a shot at a seat on an Apollo flight on down the line. In a way, it was the shittiest sort of opportunism and, to his eternal credit, Buzz never tried to deflect or shy away from the suggestion that in a strictly professional sense he had benefitted enormously from the deaths of See and Bassett. Nor was there any need for him to apologize for it. All of the astronauts (and cosmonauts for that matter) were playing one of the most dangerous games ever devised in peacetime and Buzz had risked his life in the conduct of it just like everyone else. If fate had favored him, then that was simply the luck of the draw and in no way his fault.

Buzz was born Edwin Eugene Aldrin Jr. on January 20, 1930 in Montclair, N.J.. He famously acquired his lifelong nickname as a toddler when his sister, unable to quite pronounce the word brother, took to calling little Edwin "Buzzer." The family then shortened that to Buzz and it stuck. Buzz's father, Edwin E. "Gene" Aldrin, Sr. was a commercial aviation pioneer of some renown who counted among his friends men with names like Orville Wright, Charles Lindbergh and Jimmy Doolittle. There was no mistaking the fact that Gene had aspirations for Buzz. Still, with a certain type of father, there often develops a fine line between pushing a son to achieve his potential and living vicariously through the boy. Staying on the appropriate side of that line was something Gene Aldrin would struggle with for the rest of his life. Given those circumstances, it was hardly surprising that Buzz was always eager to please his father. For example, although Buzz was enamored with football as a boy, Gene encouraged him to concentrate instead on academic pursuits and the younger Aldrin dutifully complied. His achievements were such that Buzz was able to secure an appointment to West Point where he obtained a B.S. and graduated third in a class of 435 in 1951.

Buzz then cut his aviation teeth in the Air Force flying 66 combat missions in Korea in the F-86. However, rather than go to test pilot school as many of his future colleagues at NASA had done, Buzz decided to pursue a post-graduate degree at the Massachusetts Institute of Technology (MIT). In 1963, Buzz obtained a doctorate in astronautics and aeronautics. His thesis was entitled "Guidance for Manned Orbital Rendezvous." There the trail took an interesting turn. Now too old for test pilot school, the Air Force assigned Buzz to their space systems division in Los Angeles. From there, he was assigned to the Air Force's detachment at the Space Center in Houston where he was to work on military experiments to be tested during Gemini—like the AMU. Seeing theory turned into application at NASA was the realization of every MIT egghead's dream. So Buzz threw his hat into NASA's ring and the agency brought him in to try out for a slot in Group 3. In later years, Wally Schirra would delight in recounting the story of Buzz's Group 3 interview which he conducted along with Gus Grissom. When Buzz walked into the interview room, he was wearing a tie clip with a little gold chain attached below it. Hanging from the chain were tiny gold Air Force wings and next to them dangled a Phi Beta Kappa key. Gus—and it just had to be Gus—eyed Buzz up and growled "Aldrin, we've already read your goddamn résumé, why the hell are you wearing it?" Not long after he got the Group 3 slot Buzz was saddled with the nickname "Dr. Rendezvous" which was a hybrid that incorporated his doctorate from MIT and the subject of his thesis. Despite some later (purely fictional) representations to the contrary, it was neither an expression of admiration or respect. It was the fighter jocks' way of sticking it in Buzz's ass. For Buzz's part, he was just as disdainful of what he termed their lack of "intellectual curiosity" as they were of what they perceived to be Buzz's arrogance.

It also didn't take Buzz long to earn the title of the guy no one wanted to be seated next to at a dinner party. As people with stratospheric IQs sometimes tend to be, Buzz could occasionally be clueless in matters of simple etiquette while also possessing an alarming lack of tact. Think Sheldon Cooper. There was the oft-told story of the astronaut couple who, upon hearing that Buzz's wife Joan had taken their children on an out–of–town trip, graciously invited Buzz to their home one evening for dinner. Only a problem arose when the astronaut husband got hung up at work and wasn't going to be able to make it home at the appointed time. Thinking she could head Buzz off at the pass, the astronaut wife met Buzz on her front porch and politely explained the reason for her husband's absence. Gathering that Buzz did not seem to be offended by her husband not being there, the wife's brief sense of relief was suddenly dashed when Buzz just brushed by her into the house, uncorked the bottle of wine under his arm and then proceeded to regale her with an uninterrupted three hour soliloquy on orbital mechanics and spacecraft rendezvous. Not being versed in such idle dinnertime chit-chat as astrophysics and quantum theory, Mrs. Astronaut must have felt like a lightning bug in a jar as she sat dutifully nodding her head when Buzz's lips stopped moving only to agonizingly watch them start forming words again. When the news of her ordeal got around, a lot of folks in the astronaut community thought the poor dear should have gotten a NASA Distinguished Service Medal for not setting her curtains on fire just to give herself an excuse to run screaming out of the house.

Unfortunately, Buzz's penchant for not recognizing boundaries was not limited to social situations. By mid-1965 he was becoming increasingly frustrated by not knowing where he stood in Slayton's grand scheme of things. Buzz thought that NASA ought to be more like West Point where cadets were graded out on a daily basis and where there were constant tangible criteria by which performance could be measured. Here at NASA it seemed more like a popularity contest in which assignments were handed out based upon who could contrive the most creative ways to kiss Deke and Al's asses. So Buzz asked for a meeting with Deke during which he pitched his credentials to the boss. When Buzz got finished, Deke ended the meeting with a curt, "Buzz, I'll take this matter under consideration." Blitzing Deke like that was a gutsy move but it also had the potential to blow back on Buzz. Three months later, when the crew assignments for the final Gemini missions were announced, the boomerang hit him right in the back of the head. Backup pilot for Gemini X. Buzz later had the self-awareness to admit that the move had been "arrogant" and that "I'd shafted myself." Still, he'd kept to his assigned duties and proceeded to keep his head down and his mouth shut. Then fate intervened. Buzz Aldrin would fly in the Gemini program after all.

Gemini XII would have a fully-loaded flight plan similar to every mission since Gemini VII. As before, there would be rendezvous maneuvers, docking maneuvers and the use of the Agena's capabilities while the vehicles were conjoined. But make no mistake about it, everyone at NASA knew that Gemini XII had only one true primary mission objective and that was to prove that an EVA outside the spacecraft could successfully be accomplished. In order to make that happen, NASA had to first change their underlying philosophy and overall approach to the problem. Rather than focusing on what particular tasks an astronaut could perform outside the spacecraft, they turned their attention instead to the more basic issue of understanding the mechanics of EVA itself. In turn, this required an adjustment to both how future astronauts would train for EVA *and* the type of equipment those astronauts would employ to enable themselves to function physically in a productive manner outside the spacecraft.

First came modifications to the training procedures. To this point, NASA's EVA training had involved three separate and distinct methodologies: (1) there was a pulley system which involved rigging the astronaut to wires in all fields of motion to simulate zero gravity conditions; (2) the parabolic flights of the Vomit Comet which could actually create zero-G conditions for 15 to

40 second intervals; and (3) the oversized air hockey table which could hover the astronaut over a limited surface area. Each of the three had obvious flaws. The pulley system was awkward and clunky and no matter how tightly they trussed up the astronaut he still had a tendency to gravitate downward. The Vomit Comet could produce an actual zero-G environment but NASA had to face the fact that forty seconds just wasn't enough time to perform any sort of meaningful task especially when the first few seconds invariably involved the astronaut floating straight to the top of the cabin and bonking his helmeted head on the ceiling and then having to regain his bearings. Finally, the air hockey table accomplished little more than levitating the astronaut face down in a space limited by the size of the surface area of the table.

There simply had to be a better way and, after scratching its collective head for years, NASA finally happened upon it. The oh-so elusive answer? Underwater neutral buoyancy training. Down through the years, there has been some debate about who actually came up with the idea. Some have credited Scott Carpenter who had in fact convinced NASA to put the Mercury astronauts through UDT scuba training. But in the context of the time, that really was more about preparing the astronauts for emergencies during the recovery phase of those early missions. EVA had scarcely been given a thought at that point. Another bit of folklore was that Buzz "threw a Gemini capsule into a swimming pool and then went in after it." Whatever idiosyncrasies Buzz may have had, dishonesty certainly was not one of them and he wasn't having any part of that story. While Buzz would go on to become an EVA pioneer, as to the notion that he alone devised neutral buoyancy training, Buzz flatly denied it was his idea with a blunt "Not mine." Regardless of who hit upon the idea, it was a stroke of genius. Experimentation showed that with weights properly distributed throughout the Gemini EVA spacesuit, zero gravity could be precisely simulated underwater. Only with this mode of training, the astronaut could practice EVA exercises for hours at a time. An added bonus in training for Gemini XII was that Lovell could actually sit on the edge of the pool with his legs dangling in the water and maintain a comm link with Buzz working outside the submerged spacecraft down below his feet—adding yet another layer of realism to the simulation.

Of course, developing a system to teach astronauts how to maintain control of the mass of their bodies was only part of the new EVA equation. All too often on previous EVAs, astronauts had found themselves floating or tumbling out of control, out of position relative to the spacecraft or the Agena or attempting to perform tasks that required the use of two hands while only being able to muster the use of one. NASA had equipped previous Gemini spacecraft with handrails and foot restraints but they obviously had not done the job and Aldrin's work in the pool helped to further demonstrate exactly how inadequate the prior equipment had been. When Cernan had gone outside on Gemini IX, there had been nine assistive devices on the exterior of the ship designed to help Geno both maneuver and restrain himself. By the time Buzz threw the hatch open on Gemini XII, there would be forty four. Among them would be loops for tethers that Buzz could connect to a link on either side of the waistband of his suit which would serve to anchor his core as well as a modified pair of foot restraints in the adapter section which would be dubbed "the golden slippers." Buzz might pull everything off as planned when he got outside the spacecraft or he might not but unlike any of the guys who'd gone out there before him at least Buzz was going out there with a fighting chance.

In addition to his many other fine qualities, Jim Lovell was always good for a laugh. As he and Aldrin approached the gantry elevator for the ride up to Gemini XII, the NASA press corps noticed that each of the two astronauts had a cardboard sign taped to the back of his spacesuit. "The" read Lovell's while Buzz's said "End." Once aboard, the crew could physically feel the liftoff of the Agena at Pad 14 just up the beach at 2:08 p.m. Aldrin greeted the launch of Gemini XII at 3:46 p.m. with an enthusiastic, "Look out clouds, here we come!" Almost as soon as the Titan was out of sight, crews moved in to dismantle the gantry so that it could be broken down and sold for scrap metal. Obviously, NASA wasn't long on sentimentality. Having achieved an orbit of 87 by 152 miles, Buzz advised at 1:25:50 that they'd gotten a solid radar lock on the Agena as soon as they'd turned it on. If ESPN football analyst Lee Corso had been in Mission Control that day he may have felt compelled to say, "Not so fast, my friend" because an hour later, about 64 miles out from the Agena, the onboard radar dropped out completely. Over the course of the next hour when matters hadn't improved, Buzz swung into action. It was the irony of ironies. The rendezvous radar was dead but the MIT brainiac who'd written the doctoral thesis on orbital mechanics just happened to be in the cockpit. Using only a sextant, some starcharts he'd helped to compile and what was inside his noggin (the "Mark One cranium computer", Buzz called it), he brought Gemini XII right up next to the Agena as if he'd done it a hundred times before. If Buzz at that moment was thinking, "Dr. Rendezvous THAT, bitches," then the stick and rudder guys were just gonna have to bite the bullet and give him that one.

At 3:45:47, Lovell called out "Lafayette, we are here." Twenty five minutes later, CSQ Capcom gave them a go for docking. After taking a couple of minutes to get themselves configured and for Buzz to film the sequence Lovell moved in and called, "We are docked" at 4:13:52. Eighteen minutes later, they were undocked. While Buzz was maneuvering around the Agena getting ready to try his hand at docking, Houston Capcom advised that Mission Control had observed an anomaly with the turbine pump of the Agena's Primary Propulsion System (PPS) which was the rocket that they would use for orbital maneuvers. Buzz went ahead and did his thing but at 6:09:02 Hawaii Capcom made it official. There would be no ride on the Agena PPS for Gemini XII. Somewhere, Pete Conrad just had to be dancing a jig and laughing his gap-toothed ass off because his old Pax River pal "Shaky" Lovell wasn't going to get the chance to go up and break Pete's altitude record. Pete'd get to hang onto it just a little while longer—at least until Apollo really got rolling. Onboard, after a fuel cell purge, at 7:43:32 the crew called it quits on day one.

Day two reacquisition occurred at 14:42:31. It began with some photographic work and, in particular, the photographing of an eclipse. The real work on day two was to be Buzz's first EVA. Cabin depressurization began at 19:23:00 and six minutes later, Buzz greeted the hatch opening with a "Man, look at that!" While he was floating free with his feet just above the seat, Lovell offered "What did I tell you, Buzz? Four day's vacation with pay, seeing the world." So, like any self-respecting tourist, Buzz started wearing out the Hasselblad relentlessly taking photographs of star fields. Two hours into the EVA, Buzz was so comfortable that the static electricity causing blue sparks to jump between the fingers of his glove didn't even concern him. At 21:51:00, he was back inside and the crew had experienced no difficulty getting him in or closing the hatch. So far so good. After a fuel cell purge and an update from Mission Control which included that day's Army and Navy football scores (thankfully both had won), the crew signed off on day two at 29:28:10.

Day three reacquisition occurred at 36:49:29 and it was the day that Gemini XII had to put up or shut up. The day's primary task was going to be Buzz's EVA outside the spacecraft and this was the big one. At 42:51:06 Buzz signaled that the hatch was fully open and five minutes later he was all the way out. After deploying a camera on a mount and moving up and down hand-rails on the spacecraft, Buzz hooked up his waist tether and moved over to attach the gravity gradient tether to the Agena. Buzz's underwater training was really paying off as he was breathing normally and his body temperature was nominal. He even observed at one point that his fingers and feet were actually cold. At 43:17:36 Buzz was feeling so good that he razzed Houston Capcom with a "Go Army, Beat Navy" cheer while Lovell had taken to calling him "Buzzeroni." Buzz then glided back to the adapter section and slid his feet into the golden slippers. At approximately forty minutes outside, Buzz was on cruise control. By this time on Gemini XI, Gordon was already exhausted and back inside the spacecraft. From there, Buzz leaned back parallel from the adapter section and once he'd stood back up he performed some basic tasks like using a wrench to tighten and loosen bolts and cutting straps with a scissor-like device. During that time, he had worked while on two waist tethers, then one and then while floating free. Not once did he fog over or begin to sweat into his eyes. At 44:42:26, after Buzz had wiped off Lovell's hatch window, Jim joked, "Would you change the oil too?" Fifteen minutes later, Buzz was back inside and cabin repressurization had started. Buzz had triumphantly—and brilliantly—pulled off the Gemini program's EVA tour-de-force. After a thankfully uneventful go at the tethered spacecraft/gravity centrifuge, at 51:51:24 Lovell rogered that they'd blown the tether. After a meal, it was lights out on day three at 53:17:57.

Day four began at 60:47:10. Six hours later, Buzz would pop the hatch and perform his final EVA. This was a fairly routine photographic exercise and trash dump maneuver that took about fifty three minutes. Back inside, Buzz wanted to dump his visor and threatened to reopen the hatch to do so. Lovell ordered him to keep it as a souvenir. From that point on, the crew had to nurse the fuel cells (which had been a bit balky throughout the flight) to keep the ship aloft for the scheduled number of orbits in the flight plan. By seventy hours Mission Control was piping up music to keep up the crew's morale. When Capcom Pete Conrad later added "The Sound of Music" by Julie Andrews to the soundtrack, they must have been desperate. Either that or Pete was really giving Shaky the business. Day four sign off took place at 78:33:12.

Finally, it was time to bring the guys home. Day five reacquisition took place at 84:49:32. After a flight plan update and a meal, it was time for the crew to start preparing to come down. At 92:22:00 they got an unexpected treat from Houston when Capcom radioed up "and, by the way, Gemini XII, Mohammed (sic) Ali sends his regards." Lovell thanked his Capcom and added, "He still is the greatest!" At 93:59:49 Lovell called retrofire and after twenty four seconds confirmed that all four retros had done their job. At 94:28:16, Lovell confirmed that reentry would be automatic and that they were right on the line. Two minutes later Buzz confirmed that the main chute was out. After being advised that the Wasp recovery forces had a visual on them, Aldrin gave a loud "Son of a gun!" on impact at 94:34:32. Mother Earth had greeted them with a rude kick in the pants but they were down. So too was the curtain on Project Gemini.

WHAT DID IT ALL mean? Years later, Gene Kranz would say "Gemini developed the tools and technologies we needed to go to the moon, but even more, Gemini was an essential step for the crews and the controllers. The culture of early Gemini operations centered on Kraft and Slayton, strong individuals who stepped up to the risks and with courage knocked them aside. In the process, they defined the leadership qualities needed for success in space. Their words were clear, their expectations high. They knew they needed to develop a second generation of leaders. They used Gemini to select and test those individuals who would carry the torch in Apollo."

As for the race to the moon, Chris Kraft later said that for the duration of the Gemini program, "The Russians did not fly even a single cosmonaut in space." Still, despite Korolev's death and accounting for the rumors of total disarray in the Soviet space program, Kraft quickly pointed out "but nobody on our side knew whether that was right or wrong. The Russians didn't announce advance plans or hold press conferences to discuss the future. We only found out what they were doing when they did it." So it would go. For while the American space program had forged ahead brilliantly during Gemini and had, at long last, chalked up some American "firsts" in space, because of the intense secrecy shrouding the Soviet program, NASA still could not be certain it was winning the race—whatever that meant at the end of 1966.

Still, in the final analysis, NASA had implemented a logical incremental plan during Gemini to get America to the moon. The path ahead was clear now and the United States had only to ride the momentum it had created using the equipment and methodology which had been tested and proven by the end of the Gemini program. And so they would—all the way to the Sea of

Tranquility. And while Apollo would be remembered as the program that ultimately accomplished John Kennedy's goal, never let it be forgotten that Project Gemini was the program that enabled the United States to overcome what had appeared at the time of Kennedy's challenge to be an insurmountable Soviet advantage in the space race and which gave the country a lead in that race that it would never relinquish. As Kraft put it, "My view is simple: Gemini bridged the technology gaps that made Apollo possible. Without Gemini, the Kennedy goal of landing a man on the moon and returning him safely to the Earth by the end of that marvelous decade would not have been accomplished." Simpler still, Project Gemini was:

# WHEN THE RACE WAS WON.

# Epilogue

NASA CHANGED FOREVER ON January 27, 1967. Flush with a brashness instilled by the Gemini program's successes, by early 1967 the NASA brass was confident that it would meet John Kennedy's goal. In fact, they were actually beginning to believe that they could do it with months to spare. It was a hubris that was about to be shattered. Gus and Ed White had been chosen along with rookie Roger Chaffee to fly the maiden voyage of the Apollo program and it was a plum assignment. Deke had never really made any bones about wanting one of his Mercury brethren to be the first man to set foot on the moon. Since he couldn't do it himself and because Big Al was also still grounded, Gus was emerging as the logical choice. If Ed and Roger could also pass this initial Apollo test, they might well end up accompanying Gus on what certainly would be a ride into the history books.

Rather than stick with McDonnell whose Mercury and Gemini spacecraft had, with the exception of Gemini VIII, performed in such an exemplary fashion, NASA had contracted the work on the Apollo Command and Service Module (CSM) to North American Aviation. Unfortunately, there had been difficulties with both the command module and North American almost from the moment the program started. Frustrated by the ship's litany of defects and North American's less than enthusiastic efforts to rectify them, Gus once hung a lemon on the spacecraft simulator after a training exercise. On January 27th, the crew was scheduled for an all-up "plugs-out" test of the command module which was perched atop an unfueled Saturn 1-B rocket on Pad 34. The night before, Gus and his crew had met with Wally Schirra's backup crew who had just finished the same test. At that meeting, Wally voiced his belief that the spacecraft "just didn't feel right."

Wally then ominously told Gus point blank, "If you have a glitch or any kind of anomaly, get the hell out of there." If only Gus had taken that advice.

Throughout the day on the 27th, Gus and the guys had been struggling with some bugs in the comm link. Several times, Gus had cursed in frustration. Then, at 6:31 p.m., a voice—probably Ed's—came crackling through Mission Control, "FIRE!", followed by "We've got a fire in the cockpit!" It was all over in a matter of seconds. Gus, the Gemini 3 commander and first man to go into space twice and Ed, the pilot of Gemini IV and first American to go EVA, became the first space veterans of the Gemini program to die. Strapped down helplessly inside a bum spacecraft from which they had no chance to escape in the event something went south. The American public identified so closely with the astronauts that the loss of any crew would have been devastating. But Gus and Ed? Goddamn, that hurt. Still, despite the horrific setback, NASA would continue to forge ahead and the team which had performed so brilliantly in Project Gemini would be crucial in taking Apollo to the surface of the moon.

JOHN YOUNG WOULD FOLLOW up his two stellar performances in Gemini with two more in the Apollo program. The apex of his NASA career was his command of the nearly flawless Apollo 16 mission during which he became the ninth man to walk on the moon. John would follow that up with another milestone in April, 1981 when he commanded Columbia on the maiden voyage of the space shuttle program. After one additional shuttle flight, John retired from NASA having become the first American to fly in space six times. It was a record that would endure well into the decades–long shuttle program.

Following the success of Gemini IV, Jim McDivitt had been fast-forwarded into the Apollo program. Upon his arrival, Deke assigned him to command what was to have been the second flight of the program, the primary objective of which was to conduct rendezvous and docking maneuvers of the Apollo command and lunar modules in Earth orbit. Because of a series of development problems with the LM at Grumman Aircraft, the vehicle's primary contractor, McDivitt and his crew of Dave Scott and Rusty Schweickart would be bumped behind Frank Borman's command of the historic first flight into lunar orbit in December, 1968. Their flight the following March would be designated as Apollo 9. Jim and his crew flew the daylights out of the mission and McDivitt certainly could have secured the command of a lunar landing flight down the line had he so desired. Instead, Jim chose to go into NASA management until his retirement from the program.

Ever since Deke had stuck him with the backup command of Gemini XII, Gordo Cooper had been, as Slayton had said, just "marking time" at NASA. Getting buried on a mission to nowhere at the end of Gemini meant that Gordo was going to be *way* behind the curve when it came time to jockey for a seat on an Apollo flight. Also, of course, any seat other than as an Apollo mission commander just wouldn't do for a Mercury hero and a Gemini commander—like Gordo—and that boxed him in even tighter. After his stint as backup commander for Apollo 10, many thought that Gordo just couldn't believe that when push came to shove his old Mercury buddies Deke and Al would screw him with his pants on and leave him standing on the sidelines when the command assignments were handed out for the final Apollo missions. After Al finally beat the Meniere's in time to jump back into the Apollo flight rotation, Gordo would find out just how misguided that belief had been. Gordon Cooper never flew in space again after Gemini V.

After knocking it out of the park on Gemini XI, Pete Conrad was right where he liked to be—sitting in the catbird seat. The way it was all shaking out it looked like Pete was going to end up with the command of the sixth scheduled Apollo flight. Man, that was just perfect. Of the missions on the Apollo drawing board, the fifth flight was scheduled to be the first lunar landing if—and only if—there were no major glitches on the first four missions and, come on, what were the chances of that happening? Of course, each of the first four flights did go flawlessly as did the fifth when Neil Armstrong put his boot down in the Sea of the Tranquility. So Pete got the command of Apollo 12—one of history's ultimate consolation prizes—and, in true Conrad style, he left his mark. Still fresh in everyone's minds, of course, was Armstrong's historic "That's one small step" quotation. Upon reaching the foot of the lunar module ladder in preparing to become the third man to set foot on the moon, the 5'6" (and ½) Pete cut loose with a loud "Whoopee!" followed by a "Man, that may have been a small one for Neil but that's a long one for me." A few years later, Pete would close out his legendary career by commanding the first Skylab mission. Pete passed away tragically in 1999 after an accident on his beloved Harley-Davidson. 69 years old and still out there tearing it up on a Harley. There has never been and will never be another like Pete Conrad. May God rest him.

Wally Schirra took command of the first manned Apollo mission, eventually designated as Apollo 7, after the deaths of Gus, Ed and Roger. Wally and his crewmates, Walt Cunningham and Donn Eisele, flew a terrific shakedown flight of the Apollo CSM. Wally, however, had announced his retirement prior to the mission and, knowing he wasn't going to fly again, was in no mood to tolerate any kind of nonsense from anyone in Mission Control. Fueling the fire was the fact that Wally had contracted a severe cold that had turned Jolly Wally into a cranky son–of–a–bitch. When it came down to showtime, Wally brought the ship home with pinpoint accuracy just like he always had. However, because of the hard feelings the flight had created inside Mission Control—and with Chris Kraft in particular—neither Cunningham or Eisele would ever fly for NASA again. When Apollo 17 splashed down ending the program in December, 1972, Wally held the distinction of being the only astronaut to have flown in each of the Mercury, Gemini and Apollo programs.

Tom Stafford got to wear the ultimate bridesmaid's dress, the command of Apollo 10, which was the final dress rehearsal for the first manned lunar landing. Along for the ride were John Young and Gene Cernan. The primary mission objective was to fly to the moon and then attempt rendezvous and docking maneuvers in lunar orbit for the first time in order to simulate as closely as possible a flight of the LM coming up off the surface of the moon. Despite a few dicey moments while flying the vehicle, Tom and Gene pulled it off with Young's help and thus paved the way for the Apollo 11 landing. In order to stave off any temptation that Tom may have had about perhaps heading on down to the lunar surface and grabbing the brass ring for himself and Cernan, NASA had short-fueled the ascent stage of the LM. So if they did go down and land against orders, they'd stay on the moon as a permanent monument to the space program. Though he was an absolute ace in the cockpit and one of NASA's finest astronauts, Tom would have to settle for making it to within 47,000 feet of the finish line. Fate—and NASA—would allow him no more than that in the race to the moon. Tom would later command the American side of the Apollo/Soyuz joint docking flight with the Soviets in 1975 closing out his distinguished career at NASA.

Every indignity that Frank Borman had endured during his two weeks aboard Gemini VII was to be handsomely rewarded during Project Apollo. After he was named commander of what was originally scheduled to be the third flight of the program, Lady Luck patted Borman right on the top of his square head. Partly because of development problems with the LM but mostly because they were hearing Russian footsteps, the NASA brass made two crucial changes to the flight that would end up being designated as Apollo 8. First, it would be bumped up a slot ahead of McDivitt's Earth orbit CSM/LM rendezvous flight. Second, and far more importantly, what was initially to have been just a high Earth orbit flight to test reentry procedures and the reliability of the heat shield was changed to the first flight to the moon. Since the LM was not yet ready for flight, the primary mission objective was to complete ten orbits of the moon in the CSM then blast out of orbit and return home. It was a tremendous leap of faith and one of the prime missions of the program. Conrad and Gordon had gone up to 850 miles on Gemini XI. Borman, Jim Lovell and Bill Anders would cover the last 239,150 miles to the moon. Although he had to battle extreme nausea on the way out, Frank fulfilled his command brilliantly and one of the great voyages of exploration in all of human history was successfully completed in December, 1968. Even now, fifty years later, the crew's reading from the Book of Genesis while in lunar orbit on Christmas Eve remains one of the most wonderful and nostalgic moments of the second half of the 20th century. Apollo 8 would be Frank Borman's last spaceflight. Maybe he thought he simply couldn't top it.

Jim Lovell thought he could top it and was delighted after Apollo 8 when he was slotted for command of the third lunar landing mission designated as Apollo 13. Jim's euphoria came to an abrupt halt roughly two and a half days into the flight. So much has been written (and filmed) about Jim Lovell's final NASA mission that nothing more can usefully be added here. Suffice to say that the most successful aspect of the mission—the crew's survival—was due in no small measure to the steady unflappable demeanor of the flight's commander. At the time of his retirement from NASA, Jim Lovell had spent more time in space than any other human being.

On July 20, 1969, Neil Armstrong fulfilled his destiny and became the first human being to set foot on another celestial body. As long as humanity survives and retains the intellectual capability to understand its history, Neil's name will be both remembered and revered. In many ways, Armstrong had been the perfect man to handle the acclaim that came with his achievements on Apollo 11. Quiet and introspective, Neil was never—ever—given to hyperbole and when he did speak he sounded a lot more like an engineering professor than a fighter jock. Some found his reticence annoying; others, particularly those who found it frustrating that Neil never would (if he even could) articulate how it *felt* when he took that first step even thought that he was being selfish. Those people would do well to remember that Neil didn't ask for the command of Apollo 11—Deke assigned him to the position— and, further, once he got the command he didn't actively campaign to be the first guy to step out in the way that Gene and Buzz

Aldrin (mostly Gene) had actively sought to influence the NASA brass that the honor should go to Buzz. Moreover, once the task befell him, Neil performed it flawlessly. No one has ever dared to question that. And that alone surely earned Neil the right to deal with the aftermath of the achievement in whatever way he saw fit and to let history decide the rest. So it shall. The first man to walk on the moon left the first celestial body upon which he set foot on August 25, 2012.

Dave Scott, Neil's crewmate on the perilous flight of Gemini VIII, would go on to have a brilliant career at NASA as well. After serving as McDivitt's command module pilot on the highly successful Apollo 9 mission, Dave would go on to command a fantastic lunar surface exploration on Apollo 15. The flight was noteworthy for being the first mission to employ the lunar rover, a dune buggy-like contraption that was folded up and stowed on the LM and then was brought out and unfolded on the surface of the moon. While the three previous lunar explorations had been limited to walking distance from the LM, with the rover the astronauts could trek as far as five miles away from their lunar base. It greatly enhanced the crew's ability to collect a far more varied sampling of lunar surface geology and Scott and his LM pilot Jim Irwin hit the mother lode when they found the so-called "Genesis rock" which was carbon-dated upon its return to Earth and found to be 4.2 billion—with a "b"—years old.

Following his Apollo 10 flight to the moon as Stafford's LMP, Gene Cernan was offered the same position on John Young's Apollo 16 flight, meaning that if the mission was successful Geno would become the tenth man to walk on the moon. Cernan flatly refused the assignment. Instead, he opted to gamble on his belief that he should be named the mission commander of Apollo 17. Given his NASA résumé at that time, it wasn't exactly the smartest bet in the world. For while Geno was solid gold behind a microphone and could schmooze the socks off of even the most jaded Cape reporter, his body of work at NASA to that point had hardly been stellar. First, there was the miserably failed EVA on Gemini IX. Then, when the LM went into a wild gyration while flying free in lunar orbit on Apollo 10, Geno had screamed "Son of a bitch!" over an open comm link—an epithet that was heard loud and clear by everyone from LBJ to Queen Elizabeth II to Pope Paul VI. It wasn't exactly the personification of the squeaky clean and cool-under-fire astronaut image that NASA was trying to promote in those days. Despite those things, Deke still seemed to be leaning hard toward handing Geno the far left couch on 17. So, on top of the world and out "training" at the Cape for Apollo 14 as Shepard's backup in an H-13 Bell helicopter, Geno happened upon some of Central Florida's finest out sunbathing along the banks of the Indian River. Eager to impress his bikini-clad audience while simultaneously affording himself the ultimate bird's eye view, Geno decided to go ahead and flathat the ladies. Unfortunately, during the attempt, Geno misjudged his altitude and slammed the chopper into the water. While he somehow—miraculously—managed to avoid being decapitated on impact, Geno still damn near drowned before he got himself unharnessed and up to the surface. Afterward, sitting in Slayton's office looking like a border collie who'd been fished out of the ocean after leaping off an exploding oil rig, Geno thought he'd blown the command and the walk on the moon. He got the relief of a lifetime when Deke just blew the whole thing off with a figurative headshake and a "Goddamn Geno." In truth, had Cernan screwed up like that earlier in the program, it probably would've been the end of the line for him. That he weathered it when he did likely had a lot more to do with the senioritis that had crept into the program after the cancellation of Apollos 18 through 20 than with any desire on Deke's part to indulge Cernan. Anyway, Geno kept the command and got his moonwalk while doing a superb job on Apollo 17. At the conclusion of the mission's lunar surface activity, Cernan had achieved the distinction of becoming the last man in the 20th century to leave his footprints on the surface of the moon. There were some guys at NASA, it seemed, who just couldn't buy a break in the space program. Not Gene Cernan. Geno could've shit into a tin horn and gold nuggets would have fallen out the other end.

Mike Collins, the renaissance man, fell on some difficult times after his sparkling success on Gemini X. Mike had always been as thin as a rail and athletic enough to have been considered the best handball player in the astronaut corps. That's why it was as scary as hell when in the months after X he began experiencing some very odd physical symptoms including having difficulty moving his legs. Already assigned to Borman's Apollo crew along with Anders, Collins would have to bow out in order to have spinal fusion surgery on his neck. When Apollo 8 turned out to be humankind's most historic voyage since Fourteen Hundred and Ninety Two, the situation was beginning to look like a horrible cut of the cards for Mike Collins. But Slayton, being the great boss that he was, empathized with Mike and immediately assigned him to the prime crew of Apollo 11 once the NASA medics cleared him to return to flight status. As it turned out, that flight would make some history as well and Mike Collins had a crucial role in making it.

Remember that part about the guys who just couldn't seem to catch a break in the space program? Take a bow Dick Gordon. After barely missing the cut for Group 2, he'd been one of the darlings of Group 3 and the fourth of the fourteen to be assigned to a prime crew. Plus, he'd flown on Gemini XI and that had to position him well for Apollo, right? Gordon had fairly well hitched his wagon to Conrad's and when Pete got the command of Apollo 12 he was never not gonna take Dickie-Dickie with him. Then, when their crewmate C.C. Williams was killed in a freakish T-38 crash, Pete brought Group 3's Alan Bean aboard to replace him. But instead of Dick sliding over to the LMP seat and getting to take Apollo 12's moonwalk with Pete, Bean got that slot which left Dick circling above them in lunar orbit. Prior to closing the hatch before LM separation Dick looked at Bean and thought "I wish that son-of-a-bitch fit three people." But no matter, right? Gordon got the command of Apollo 18 and he'd get his moonwalk on that mission. Of course, Congress then canceled Apollo 18. Yeah, if it weren't for bad luck, Dick Gordon wouldn't have had any luck at all.

Then there was Dr. Rendezvous. Buzz Aldrin had absolutely EVA'd his butt off on Gemini XII. But, because of the fact that no one in either NASA's administration or the Astronaut Office was particularly crazy about him, that achievement didn't really guarantee him much. Luckily for Buzz, Neil Armstrong was one of the few people in Houston or at the Cape that he hadn't rubbed the wrong way. When Deke almost sheepishly floated the idea of flying with Buzz to Neil, Armstrong pretty much just shrugged his shoulders as if to say "Why not?" It was a manifestation of one of Armstrong's many exceptional qualities. First, Neil didn't give a hoot if everyone else at NASA had the perception that Buzz was a jerk. Until he saw that for himself, Neil wasn't going to make a judgment based upon rumors or someone else's opinion. Second, even if the stories were true, he was in command and wasn't about to take any crap from Buzz or anyone else assigned to his crew. Neil would give him a fair shake and if Buzz couldn't hack it, he'd kick his ass off. Period. As it turned out, Neil Armstrong ended up being a godsend for Buzz Aldrin. Even with the flap over who'd get out first, Buzz managed not to mess up his working relationship with Neil and Buzz's reward was the second footprint on the moon. Hell, he'd even have a character in "Toy Story" named after him. Of course, the rest was a mixed bag. After struggling for years with alcoholism which he believed had been misdiagnosed as depression, Buzz dealt with the fame that Apollo 11 had bestowed upon him with varying degrees of success at various stages of his life. And don't think for a minute that during the rough patches that some of his former NASA colleagues didn't have a snicker or two at Dr. Rendezvous' expense. Some of those guys might have been more inclined to cut Buzz some slack if they'd known more about him. As previously recounted, at the time of his matriculation from West Point, Buzz had ranked third in a class of 435 cadets. Relatively few fathers have or ever will experience the pride and gratification of having a son graduate from the United States Military Academy. Far fewer still have had or will know the feeling of having a son leave that revered institution with a class rank that rivaled those of Robert E. Lee and Douglas MacArthur—like

Buzz's did. Gene Aldrin's reaction to his son ranking third in his West Point class was something akin to "Son, we Aldrins don't celebrate a bronze medal." The elder Aldrin had a similar reaction when Buzz became "only" the second man to walk on the moon. Men have said and done far worse things than anything Buzz Aldrin ever said or did over a hell of a lot less than that.

As they used to say in the Old West, Deke Slayton would've drank turpentine and pissed on a brushfire if it would've gotten the NASA medics off his back and gotten him back into the flight line. Unfortunately for Deke, that would not happen during the lunar exploration phase of the Apollo program. By 1975, maybe the heart issue had finally gone away or maybe NASA just thought they owed it to him but Deke got assigned to the last Apollo flight which was the joint docking mission with the Soviets that came to be designated as the Apollo/Soyuz Test Project (ASTP). Because he'd been grounded for thirteen years, NASA couldn't just hand Deke the keys so he had to fly second seat to Stafford. By that point, it was highly likely that Deke didn't give a damn about getting a command. It was enough that he'd finally get his ride and, of course, he did a great job—just like he always knew he would.

After seven long years in astronaut purgatory, Big Al Shepard would reemerge after having had what was at the time an experimental surgery of the inner ear to repair his Meniere's syndrome. Then, with Slayton's invaluable help and backing, Al seized—literally—the command of Apollo 14. Of course, there was a chorus of complaints alleging favoritism and finger-pointing about Al's lack of spaceflight experience. Fortunately for Al, that sort of chatter was another thing Deke Slayton didn't give a damn about. Shepard was going to the lunar surface as the standard-bearer for Project Mercury and that's all there was to it. When he finally got there, Al attached the clubhead of a six iron to the handle for the contingency sample scoop, plopped down a golf ball and hit the first "sandtrap shot" on the moon. Later in life, Shepard told the story of having a post–Apollo 14 brandy with his father when the elder Shepard asked him if Alan remembered his reaction when Alan first informed him that he was going to be an astronaut.

"Yes sir, I do" Shepard recounted, "You were not in favor of it." After which his father raised his glass and said, "I was wrong." Big Al, choked with emotion and eyes brimming with tears recalled, "That's all he needed to say." Shepard had been there since day one. Had seen and done it all. Had inhaled the fame and the adulation. Had helped himself to the Corvettes and the Cape cookies. Had even walked on the fucking moon. Yet, for all his mercurial behavior and alleged complexity, at the end of the line the validation that mattered most—perhaps the only validation that mattered at all—to Alan B. Shepard, Jr. was being told that he was a good son and that he'd done a good job. By Alan B. Shepard, Sr.—The Colonel.

Eventually, Gene Kranz knew, he would have to bid farewell to and let go of the flight director's console that had become part of his soul and move to the back row of Mission Control just as Chris Kraft had done before him. Knowing that he had to do it didn't make doing it any easier. When the time came, Kranz never blinked or equivocated—as if a man like Gene Kranz was even capable of doing either of those things—when stating that his days as a flight director were the most happy and fulfilling of his life. And what times they had been. Gene was on console when Neil and Buzz touched down in the Sea of Tranquility. That alone would have been enough to make an extraordinary career but his legend grew even larger due to his critical role in the rescue of Apollo 13 and the recovery of its crew. In October, 1993, at Indiana University's Southeast Campus in New Albany, Gene held hundreds in his audience spellbound as he recounted the timeline of the Apollo 13 mission. This guy—THIS GUY—was the personification of the America those people remembered from that time now long ago. That bygone America that they yearned for. The guy who said that when America takes on a job, "Failure is not an option" and meant it with every ounce of his being. Sadly, in our nation's Capital today, failure in the U.S. space program is viewed not only as an option but as business as usual. Shame on them and on each and every one of us for letting them get away with it. Because we owe guys like Gene Kranz and his flight controllers so much better than that.

At the time this work was completed, Christopher Columbus Kraft, Jr. still survives. He will be 95 years old on February 28, 2019. With the passing of John Glenn, he is the last living icon of Project Mercury. There is an age-old debate over whether extraordinary times compel ordinary men to do extraordinary things or if extraordinary men mold the times in which they live. If it is the latter, let us hope that a future American generation will produce another Chris Kraft. A brilliant and fearless innovator around whom will be built the team that will light the path for the next great American enterprise. The one that will lead our country back to the forefront of mankind's exploration of the heavens. America, after all, should never accept less than greatness. Godspeed Flight—and thank you.

## THE END

# Bibliography

## Mission Transcripts

NASA Johnson Space Center Info > History Portal

### Gemini 3

www.JSC.NASA.gov/History/Mission-trans/Gemini3.htm

GTO3 TEC PDF

Gemini 3 Composite air to ground, ground to air and onboard voice tape transcription, 107 pages

### Gemini IV

www.JSC.NASA.gov/History/Mission-trans/Gemini4.htm

GT04 TEC PDF

Gemini IV Composite air to ground, ground to air and onboard voice tape transcription, 398 pages

### Gemini V

www.JSC.NASA.gov/History/Mission-trans/Gemini5.htm

GTO5 TE2 PDF

Gemini V Composite air to ground, ground to air and onboard voice tape transcription, 784 pages

## Gemini VI

HTTPS: www.JSC.NASA.gov/History/Mission-trans/Gemini6.htm

GT06 TEC PDF

## Gemini VII

HTTPS: www.JSC.NASA.gov/History/Mission-trans/Gemini7.htm

GT07 061 PDF

Volumes 1-3

Gemini VII Composite air to ground, ground to air and onboard voice tape transcription, Volume 1     338 pages

Gemini VII Composite air to ground, ground to air and onboard voice tape transcription, Volume 2     338 pages

Gemini VII Composite air to ground, ground to air and onboard voice tape transcription, Volume 3     338 pages

1015 total pages

## Gemini VIII

HTTP: www.JSC.NASA.gov/History/Mission-trans/Gemini8.htm

GT08 TEC PDF

Gemini VIII Composite air to ground, ground to air and onboard voice tape transcription, 113 pages

## Gemini IX

HTTP: www.JSC.NASA.gov/History/Mission-trans/Gemini9.htm

GT09A2 TEC PDF

Gemini IX Composite air to ground, ground to air and onboard voice tape transcription, 349 pages

### *Gemini X*

HTTP: www.JSC.NASA.gov/History/Mission-trans/Gemini10.htm

GT10 TEC PDF

Gemini X Composite air to ground, ground to air and onboard voice tape transcription, 338 pages

### *Gemini XI*

HTTP: www.JSC.NASA.gov/History/Mission-trans/Gemini11.htm

GT11 TEC PDF

Gemini XI Composite air to ground, ground to air and onboard voice tape transcription, 345 pages

### *Gemini XII*

HTTP: www.JSC.NASA.gov/History/Mission-trans/Gemini12.htm

GT12 TEC PDF

Gemini XII Composite air to ground, ground to air and onboard voice tape transcription, 497 pages

## Johnson Space Center—Biographical Data

Buzz Aldrin httds://www.jsc.nasa.gov/Bios/htmlbios/Aldrin-b. html

Dick Gordon httds://www.jsc.nasa.gov/Bios/htmlbois/ Gordon-RF.

Gene Cernan httds://www.jsc.nasa.gov/Bios/htmlbois/ Cernan-EA.

Tom Stafford httds://www.jsc.nasa.gov/Bios/htmlbois/ Stafford-TP.

Gus Grissom httds://history.nasa.gov/apollo204/zorn/grissom. htm

John Young httds://www.jsc.nasa/gov/Bios/htmlbois/Young

Jim McDivitt httds://www.jsc.nasa/gov/Bios/htmlbois/ McDivit-JA.

Ed White httds://www.jsc.nasa/gov/Bios/htmlbois/White-EH.

Gordo Cooper httds://www.jsc.nasa/gov/Bios/htmlbois/ Cooper-LG.

Pete Conrad httds://www.jsc.nasa.gov/Bios/htmlbois/Conrad-C.

Wally Schirra httds:www.jsc.nasa.gov/Bios/htmlbois/ Schirra-WM.

Jim Lovell httds:www.jsc.nasa.gov/Bios/htmlbois/Lovell-JA.

Frank Borman httds:www.jsc.nasa.gov/Bios/htmlbois/Borman-F.

Neil Armstrong httds:www.jsc.nasa.gov/Bios/htmlbois/ Armstrong-NA.

Dave Scott httds:www.jsc.nasa.gov/Bios/htmlbois/Scott-DR.

Mike Collins

https://en.wikipedia.org/wiki/michael_collins_(Astronaut)

Chris Kraft

https://en.wikipedia.org/wiki/christopher_c._kraft_jr

## Books

Aldrin, Buzz and Malcolm McDonnell. *Men from Earth*. 2nd ed. New York Bantam Falcon Books, 1991. Hereinafter "Aldrin"

Apogee Mission Reports

Gemini 4, 6, 7, 12 Ontario: Apogee books

IV-2011 VI-2000 VII-2002 XII-2003 Hereinafter "Mission Report"

Barbree, Jay. *Live From Cape Canaveral.* New York: Harper Collins, 2007. Hereinafter "Barbree"

Borman, Frank with Robert J. Serling. *Countdown.* New York: Morrow, 1988. Hereinafter "Borman"

Brever, William B. *Race To The Moon: America's Duel With The Soviets.* Westport, Connecticut: Praeger, 1993. Hereinafter "Brever"

Buckbee, Ed with Wally Schirra. *The Real Space Cowboys.* Ontario: Apogee Books, 2005. Hereinafter "Buckbee"

Burgess, Colin. *Selecting The Mercury Seven.* Chichester, UK: Springer-Praxis, 2011. Hereinafter "Burgess"

Burrows, William E. *This New Ocean.* New York: Random House, 1998. Hereinafter "Burrows"

Carpenter, Scott with Kris Stoever. *For Spacious Skies.* Orlando: Harcourt, 2002. Hereinafter, "Carpenter"

Carpenter, Scott, L. Gordon Cooper, Jr., John H. Glenn, Jr., Virgil I Grissom, Walter M. Schirra, Jr., Alan B. Shepard, Jr., Donald K. Slayton, *We Seven.* New York: Simon and Schuster, 1962. Hereinafter "Seven"

Cernan, Eugene with Don Davis. *The Last Man on the Moon.* New York: St. Martin's Press, 1999. Hereinafter "Cernan"

Chaikin, Andrew. *A Man on the Moon.* New York: Viking Penguin, 1994. Hereinafter "Chaikin"

Collins, Michael. *Carrying The Fire: An Astronaut's Journeys.* New York: Farrar, Strauss and Girouk, 1974. Hereinafter "Collins"

Conrad, Nancy and Howard A. Klausner. *Rocketman.* New York: New American Library, 2005. Hereinafter "Conrad"

Cooper, Gordon with Bruce Henderson. *A Leap of Faith*. New York: Harper Collins, 2000. Hereinafter "Cooper"

Cunningham, Walter. *The All American Boys*. New York: Simon and Schuster, 1977. Hereinafter "Cunningham"

French, Francis and Colin Burgess. *In The Shadow of the Moon*. Lincoln, Nebraska: University of Nebraska Press, 2007. Hereinafter "French/Burgess"

Glenn, John with Nick Taylor. *A Memoir*. New York: Bantam, 1999. Hereinafter "Glenn"

Hacker, Barton C. and James M. Grimwood. *On the Shoulders of Titans: A History of Project Gemini. NASA History Series*. Washington D.C: NASA, 1977. Hereinafter "Hacker"

Hansen, James R. *First Man: The Life of Neil Armstrong*. New York: Simon and Schuster, 2005. Hereinafter "Hansen"

Kraft, Christopher C. Jr., with James L. Schefter. *Flight*. New York: Dutton, 2001. Hereinafter "Kraft"

Kranz, Gene. *Failure Is Not An Option*. New York: Simon & Schuster, 2000. Hereinafter "Kranz"

Leopold, George. *Calculated Risk: The Supersonic Life and Times of Gus Grissom*. West Lafayette: Purdue University Press, 2016. Hereinafter "Leopold"

Lovell, Jim and Jeffrey Kluger. *Lost Moon*. New York: Houghton Mifflin, 1994. Hereinafter "Lovell"

Murray, Charles and Catherine Bly Cox. *Apollo: The Race to the Moon*. New York: Simon and Schuster, 1989. Hereinafter "Murray/Cox"

Reichl, Eugen. *Project Gemini*. (originally published as *Project Gemini*. Stuttgart, Germany: Motorbuch Verlag, 2013) Atglen, PA: Schiffer Publishing, LTD, 2016. Hereinafter "Reichl"

Schefter, James. *The Race*. New York: Doubleday/Random House, 1999. Hereinafter "Schefter"

Schirra, Walter M. Jr with Richard M. Billings. *Schirra's Space*. Boston: Quinlan, 1998. Hereinafter "Schirra"

Scott, David and Alexei Leonov. *Two Sides of the Moon*. New York: Thomas Dunne Books/St. Martin's Press, 2004. Hereinafter "Scott"

Shayler, David. *Gemini: Steps to the Moon*. Chichester UK: Springer-Praxis, 2001. Hereinafter "Shayler"

Shepard, Alan and Deke Slayton with Jay Barbree and Howard Benedict. *Moonshot*. Atlanta: Turner Publishing, 1994. Hereinafter "Shepard/Slayton"

Slayton, Donald K., with Michael Cassutt. *Deke!* New York: Tom Doherty Associates, 1994. Hereinafter "Slayton"

Stafford, Thomas P. with Michael Cassutt. *We Have Capture*. Washington, D.C.: Smithsonian Press, 2002. Hereinafter "Stafford"

Thompson, Neal. *Light this Candle*. New York: Crown Publishers, 2004. Hereinafter "Thompson"

Wendt, Guenter and Russell Still. *The Unbroken Chain*. Ontario: Apogee Books, 2001. Hereinafter "Wendt"

Whitehouse, David. *Apollo 11 The Inside Story*. London: Icon Books Ltd., 2019. Hereinafter "Whitehouse"

Wolfe, Tom. *The Right Stuff*. New York: Farrar, Strauss & Giroux, 1979. Hereinafter "Wolfe"

Young, John, W. with James R. Hansen. *Forever Young*. Gainesville: University Press of Florida, 2012. Hereinafter "Young"

## Films/Documentaries

Moon Shot: The Inside Story of the Race to the Moon—TBS
 DVD—Turner Home Entertainment (1994)
 Episode 1—Moon Fever
 Episode 2—Bridge to the Moon
 Episode 3—Go Fever
 Episode 4—"…And Never Give Up"

From the Earth to the Moon
 Part 3—We have Cleared the Tower
 Home Box Office (1998)

 Race To The Moon
 The Daring Adventure of Apollo 8
 PBS Home Video (2005)

 The Race to the Moon/History Channel
 Volume 1: Failure is Not an Option
 Documentary AAE-71302 (2004)

 When We Left Earth
 The NASA Missions
 Episode 2: Friends and Rivals
 Discovery Channel Video (2008)

 Apollo 13: To The Edge and Back
 A Thrilling Struggle Against All Odds
 WGBH/Boston Video (1994/2004)

 To The Moon
 NOVA/WGBH Video (2000)

 First Man On the Moon
 NOVA/PBS Video (2013)
 Smithsonian Dreams of Flight

To The Moon
Slingshot DVD (2003)

For All Mankind
The Criterion Collection (1999)

Spaceflight
Corporation for Public Broadcasting Volumes 1-3 (1985)

The Wonder of it All
Indican Pictures (2009)

In The Shadow of the Moon
Lionsgate Think Film (2007)

# Author's Notes

## Prologue

*Project Mercury*

P. 2 **"Bob Gilruth informed the seven astronauts."** Those seven men were: Malcolm S. "Scott" Carpenter; L. Gordon "Gordo" Cooper; John H. Glenn, Jr.; Virgil I. "Gus" Grissom; Walter M. "Wally" Schirra, Jr.; Donald K. "Deke" Slayton; Alan B. Shepard, Jr. Early NASA and Soviet space history/ Sputnik, Burrows pp. 182-183; Explorer 1, pp. 208-11; Formation of NASA, p. 218; Mercury 7, pp. 288-99; Gagarin, pp. 311-17.

P. 2 **"Named Freedom 7"** Thompson pp. 252-257. Recounts in detail Shepard's historic first flight of the Mercury program.

P. 3 **"Top of the NASA flight rotation."** Author's note: The "Ol' Pyramid" as it had been known in the flight test community since Chuck Yeager's heyday at Edwards Air Force Base in the late 1940s.

P. 3 **"As Gus himself put it"** Grissom NASA bio. p. 6. Also, Grissom's Liberty Bell 7 ordeal was recounted in Wolfe pp. 233-44 and Leopold pp. 122-123

P. 3 **"An investigation"** Author's note: Which proved to be inconclusive.

P. 4 **"Friendship 7, as Glenn dubbed it"** Glenn's account of his historic first orbital flight can be found in his memoirs, Glenn pp. 256-274, and also see, "The Lindbergh of his Time" Burrows p. 342

**P. 4 "This had prompted NASA's leadership to insist"** Kraft pp. 159-161.

**P. 4 "Come to know as Deke"** Slayton's grounding. Slayton pp. 110-113.

**P. 5 "Aurora 7, which Carpenter's mission"** Carpenter's account of his flight can be found at Carpenter pp. 256-290; Chris Kraft's account of Aurora 7, Kraft pp. 164-170.

**P. 5 "Kraft would later recall"** Quote is from Kraft interview, Moon Shot DVD Part 1 Episode 2 "Bridge to the Moon" @ 1:00:11:11.

**P. 6 "As long as Kraft had breath in his body"** Kraft p. 170.

**P. 6 "To add insult to injury"** Early space history recounted, Burrows pp. 160-166, pp. 274-284, p. 346; Scott p. 77; Slayton, p. 118.

**P. 6 "Sigma 7."** Recounted at Schirra pp. 85-90.

**P. 7 "As Slayton would say,"** Slayton p. 121.

**P. 7 "As Shepard later recounted,"** Shepard interview, Moon Shot DVD Part 1 Episode 2 @ 1:06:05.

**P. 7 "After Slayton had been grounded,"** Deke's appointment to chief of the Astronaut Office explained. Slayton pp. 115-116.

**P. 8 "Like a turd in a punch bowl"/Schirra quote/Throwing me a bone.** Moon Shot DVD Part 1 Episode 2 @ 1:04:11.

**P. 8 "Cooper rewarded"** Faith 7 recounted, Cooper pp. 41-63.

**P. 8 "Sent up Valentina Tereshkova"** Burrows pp. 346-348.

## *The Mode*

P. 9 **"Since the days of Oberth"** To The Moon DVD; Houbolt Interview @ 10:26.

P. 9 Houbolt quote, **"Down at the Cape"** To The Moon DVD @ 13:02.

P. 9 **"Houbolt happened upon"** Slayton pp. 126-127.

## *On To Gemini*

P. 12 **"Their names ...were"**

Author's note: The Group 3 astronauts would come aboard on October 14, 1963. Their names were: Edwin "Buzz" Aldrin; William Anders; Charles Bassett; Alan Bean; Eugene Cernan; Roger Chaffee; Michael Collins; Walter Cunningham; Donn Eisele; Theodore Freeman; Richard Gordon; Russell Schweickart; David Scott; and Clifton C. Williams.

P. 12 **"For Gemini, McDonnell"** Reichl, p. 101

Author's note: The primary focus of this work is to tell the story of the Gemini program through the recollections of the people most intimately involved with it. Because of that fact, detailed technical or engineering explanations and jargon have been used only when absolutely necessary; if you wish to delve further into these technical and/or engineering aspects of the Gemini program, I highly recommend Reichl's book cited in Bibliography.

P. 13, **"It was Al Shepard"** Slayton quote, Moon Shot DVD Part 1 Episode 2 @ 1:13:58.

P. 13 **"Also mischievous,"** Thompson p. 13.

P. 13 **"Eventually"** Thompson p. 19.

P. 13 **"Also, by the mid-1930's"** Thompson p. 16.

P. 13 **"Deciding not to follow"** Thompson p. 24.

P. 13 **"At Patuxent River"** Thompson pp. 105-106.

P. 13 **"He would parlay"** Thompson p. 145.

P. 13 **"He'd been accepted"** Thompson p. 165

P. 15, **"I got up to go to"** Shepard quote, Moon Shot DVD Part 1 Episode 2 @ 1:14:03.

P. 15 **"Seeing his pal in distress"** Thompson pp. 296-300.

PP. 16-17 **"The Soviets let go"/Voskhod 1 flight** Burrows pp. 350-352.


# Chapter 1: Molly

PP. 19-20 **"Virgil I. "Gus" Grissom"** All biographical information on Grissom taken from NASA Apollo One bio (pp. 1-3) and Leopold p. 18, pp. 22-23, p. 47, p. 69, p. 94.

P. 20 **"After the Liberty Bell 7 saga unfolded"** Author's note: None of the surviving Mercury astronauts ever gave much, if any, credence to Tom Wolfe's "squirmin' hatchblower" portrayal of Gus during the flight of Liberty Bell 7 in "The Right Stuff" and neither do I. There's no evidence to support it and Wolfe's florid attempt to dramatize the event stained an honorable and courageous man's name and reputation. In my opinion, it is a disgrace and both Wolfe and the producers of "The Right Stuff" movie owe Gus's family an apology.

P. 20 **"In a move that certainly"** Gus's post-Mercury career trajectory discussed quoting Shepard/Slayton p. 177; Leopold p. 166.

P. 21 **"Necessary because Gemini would not"** Slayton p. 185.

P. 21 **"The one ... Gusmobile"** Lengthy quote lifted from French/Burgess p. 4.

P. 21 **"No one in the astronaut corps,"** Lovell quote, Moon Shot DVD Part 1 Episode 2 @ 1:13:33.

PP. 21-22 **Young biographical information** taken from NASA bio p. 1 and Young p. 9, pp. 18-19, p. 22, p. 27, p. 41, p. 57.

P. 22 **"Rarely deviate throughout"** Author's note: As well as the Apollo program thereafter.

P. 23 **"Devilish notion"—Process of naming of G3 spacecraft**, French/Burgess p. 7.

P. 23 **"Uh… Titanic"** Deke p. 148; Leopold p. 165.

P. 23 **"Only mission designations"** Author's note: That rule would remain in place until Apollo 9 when the first joint flight of the CSM and LM in mission configuration—including undocking and flying free of one another-necessitated that the CSM and LM each have separate call signs. For Apollo 9, those call signs were "Gumdrop" for the CSM and "Spider" for the LM.

PP. 23-24 **"Christopher Columbus Kraft, Jr."** Kraft bio/Kraft p. 6.

P. 24 **"Acquainted with Robert R. "Bob" Gilruth"** Kraft p. 28.

P. 24 **"Invited Kraft to join"** Kraft p. 65.

P. 24 **"The job ahead"** quote, Kraft p. 67

P. 24 **"One of the earliest and most"** Early spacecraft operations discussed by Kraft; Kraft p. 78.

PP. 24-25 **Creation of Mercury Control Center.** Kraft pp. 99-102.

P. 25 **"Necessitated a backup for Kraft"** Author's note: Kraft chose John Hodge for the position.

PP. 25-26 **OAMs thrusters discussed.** Leopold p. 172.

P. 26 **"Finally, NASA had tacked on"** Experiments discussed. Hacker pp. 230-231.

P. 26 **"With the mission checklist established"** Hacker p. 232.

P. 26 **"You're on your way, Molly Brown"** Slayton p. 148.

P. 26 **"Liftoff was so smooth"/"Fire in the hole"** Young p. 79.

PP. 26-27 **Launch insertion/"Five and a half minutes"** Hacker p. 233.

P. 27 **"87 x 125 miles"** French/Burgess p. 11; Leopold p. 172.

P. 27 **"Cabin pressure gauge read zero"** Young pp. 80-81; Leopold p. 174.

P. 27 **"Mark"! at 1:33:00 (MET).** Author's note: (MET) references Mission Elapsed Time in all NASA Gemini air to ground and ground to air transmissions. From this point forward in the text, any references to time during the flight of a mission will be given in MET unless otherwise specifically noted by the author.

P. 27 **"The second firing of the OAMS"** French/Burgess p. 13; Leopold p. 178.

PP. 27-28 **"The third and final test"** Hacker p. 235; Leopold p. 178.

P. 28 **"It turned out that" Gemini 3 splashdown details recounted.** Young p. 82; Leopold p. 183.

P. 28 **"Gus then jettisoned the chutes"** Hacker p. 236.

P. 28 Molly Brown **"was no boat"** Hacker p. 237; Young p. 82.

PP. 29-30 **Sandwichgate discussed.** Young pp. 84-85; Leopold pp. 178-180.

P. 30 **"On March 18, 1965"; Leonov discusses his spacewalk on Voskhod 2.** Scott pp. 1-4; Burrows pp. 352-353

P. 31 **"One thousand mile overshoot" Voskhod 2 landing recounted.** Barbree p. 103; Shepard/Slayton pp. 173-174; Scott pp. 112-119.

## Chapter 2: The Boy Scout Takes a Walk

P. 33 **"As Deke said, "I figured""** Slayton p. 137.

P. 34 **"As to the specific factors impacting Gemini IV,"** See Prologue Note #24; Discussion of fuel cell development lifted verbatim from Shayler pp. 39-41; Along with Reichl, Shayler is an excellent reference for the engineering and/or technological aficionado.

P. 34 **"Could last no longer than four days"** Slayton p. 146.

P. 35 **"As Chris Kraft explained,"** quote. Kraft p. 127.

P. 35 **"As Kraft would point out,"** Discussion of hardware development requirements. Kraft p. 218.

P. 36 **"A former Air Force"** Kranz p. 115.

P. 36 **"As to Kranz's current assignment"** Kranz quoting Kraft; Kranz p. 134.

P. 36 **"SECO"** Author's note: In flight control jargon, first stage cut-off was referred to as booster engine cut-off or "BECO" while second stage cut-off was referred to as sustainer engine cut-off or "SECO."

P. 37 **"McDivitt was born"** McDivitt NASA bio/JSC bio and French/Burgess p. 18.

P. 37 **"Had anything bad to say about Jim"** Author's note: The fact that McDivitt wasn't a big talker surely didn't hurt.

PP. 37-38 **"Ed White was born"** White NASA bio; French/Burgess p. 19.

P. 38 **"As Slayton would later reveal"** Slayton p. 136.

PP. 38-39 **"One warm evening in Houston"** Armstrong house fire described, Hansen p. 282.

P. 39 **"Group 3 astronaut Eugene Cernan"** Cernan quote, When We Left Earth DVD Episode 2 "Friends and Rivals" @ 17:04.

P. 39 **"Shifting the locale of the nerve center"** Author's note: There had been talk of building the new Mission Control Center in California but a fellow from the Texas hill country named Lyndon Baines Johnson wasn't about to allow that to happen. Today, that center—which is still the nerve center for all American spaceflight operations—bears his name.

P. 39 **"In truth, flight operations had outgrown Mercury Control"** Kraft pp. 192-193.

PP. 39-40 **"Webb quite predictably turned to Chris Kraft"** quote, Kraft p. 192.

P. 40 **"Kraft recommended Philco"** Kraft pp. 192-193.

P. 40 **"Known as "The Trench.""** Author's note: One of the new additions to Mission Control designed to eliminate the Mercury Control runners was the inclusion of a pneumatic tube system throughout the building—like the one at your local bank's drive-through window. The "P—Tube System" as it was called, resulted in empty canisters littering the Mission Control floor. As the tubes stacked up around White team FIDO John Llewellyn, the former Marine stood up, surveyed them, and stated loudly, "I think I am back in the trenches again with my fire control team." The flight dynamics team adopted the name for its row of consoles in Mission Control and the name "The Trench" stuck. Recounted at Kranz p. 141. More about John Llewellyn later.

P. 40 **Interior layout of Mission Control discussed.** Shayler pp. 66-70.

P. 40 **"Their's was a world"** Aaron quote/Failure is Not an Option DVD @ 20:21.

PP. 40-41 **"Kranz provided these more human"** quote, Kranz p. 142.

P. 41 **"Like it or not"** Three team system discussed; Kranz p. 133.

P. 41 **"Kraft sent flight director Glynn Lunney"** Hacker p. 250.

P. 41 **"On June 3, 1965"** French/Burgess pp. 26-27.

P. 41 **"By T-minus 100 minutes"** Hacker p. 245.

P. 42 **"For the first time in the history"** Slayton p. 150.

PP. 42-43 **"Deke best described what happened next"** Quote, Slayton p. 151.

P. 43 **"In Houston, Kraft turned to Grissom,"** Kraft p. 220; French/Burgess p 28.

P. 43 **"Deke demonstrated"** Quote, Slayton p. 151.

P. 43 **"As to EVA preparation"** Quote, Hacker p. 248.

P. 44 **"Look 'tired and hot'"** Hacker p 248; French/Burgess p. 29.

P. 45 **"A design feature"** Kraft p. 221.

P. 45 **"Closing the hatch wasn't"** Kraft p. 222.

P. 46 **McDivitt quote/Drifting flight;** G IV Mission Report p. 114, p. 121.

P. 46 **"Equipped with a small onboard computer"** Hacker p. 252.

P. 47 **"Oscillations from the drogue"** Hacker p. 253.

P. 47 **"Once they'd landed, Jim asked"** French/ Burgess p. 35.

P. 47 **"None of the predicted medical"** Kraft p. 224.

P. 47 **"No reason to throw up any roadblocks"** Slayton p. 152; Kraft p. 224.

P. 48 Author's note: After Gemini 3, NASA switched the mission designation for all future Gemini flights to Roman numerals. Hence, "Geminis 3 and IV."

## Chapter 3: Eight Days in a Garbage Can

P. 49 **"To have Guenter Wendt."** Author's note: Wendt was known as the "Pad Fuhrer" among NASA personnel. He was a German refugee whose expertise at preparing space vehicles for launch was unparalleled. He also ruled the highly sanitized pre-launch area around the spacecraft's open hatches, known as the "White Room", with an iron hand.

P. 50 **"Charles Conrad Jr"** Conrad p. 19.

P. 50 **"Born to privilege"** Conrad NASA bio p. 1.

P 50, **"As a fourth grader"** Conrad p. 25.

P. 50 **"Tapped to play the Virgin Mary."** Author's note: Perhaps the most egregious example of miscasting in the entire history of American theater.

P. 50 **"Still unbroken record for demerits"** Conrad p. 53.

P. 50 **"From there, Peter headed to Princeton"** Conrad NASA bio p. 1.

PP. 51-52 **"Being such a colorful guy"** Margaret Lowell/Flying lessons, et al; Conrad pp. 54-55.

P. 52 **"Pete then made the cut"** Conrad p. 113.

P. 52 **"A totally blank white sheet of paper"** Conrad p. 116. Author's note: In reading Pete's narrative, he makes it sound as if all the testing in question—including the psychological testing—took place at the Lovelace Clinic. In reviewing other sources it is clear that the psychological testing was, in fact, performed at Wright-Patterson. It is possible that Pete didn't want the details to bog down a great story.

P. 53 **"Finally, by day eleven"** Conrad p. 118.

P. 53 **"The Albuquerque enema bag toss"** Conrad p. 127.

P. 53 **"Then, of course, there was Gordo"** Cooper NASA bio pp. 1-2.

P. 54 **"Launch day"** Cooper p. 5.

P. 54 **"Gordo was considered a "question mark""** Slayton p. 127.

P. 55 **"Rather than allow the matter"** Cooper pp. 112-113.

P. 55 **"At dinner that night"** Cooper p. 114.

P. 56 **"This time Gordo relented"** Author's note: Every mission after Gemini V would feature a mission patch which Gordo—and almost no one else—referred to as "Cooper patches".

P. 56 **"Of course, the most important"** Hacker p. 225; French/Burgess p. 42.

P. 58 **"On August 19, 1965"** Hacker p. 256; French/Burgess p. 44.

P. 58 **"All power"** Conrad quote, French/Burgess p. 45.

P. 58 **"The erector stand was brought in"** Hacker p. 256.

P. 59 **"Cadillac"** Cooper p. 119; French/Burgess p. 46.

P. 59 Gordo **"Proving"** quote, Cooper p. 120.

P. 59 **"In Mission Control"** Kraft quote; Kraft p. 230.

P. 60 **"Now, Kraft had to make a call"** Kraft p. 230.

P. 60 **"Kraft gave the order"** Kranz p. 147.

P. 60 **"A go/no-go decision"** Conrad p. 141.

P. 60 **"Using ground radar"** Kraft p. 232.

PP. 61-62 **"The romance ended"** Lengthy Conrad quote, Conrad pp. 140-141.

P. 62 **"As Kranz would later"** quote, Kranz p. 148.

P. 62 **"Kraft lit up a cigar."** Kranz p. 149.

P. 63 **First "to be guided"** quote, Cooper p. 127.

P. 63 **"The computer was"** Cooper p. 128.

P. 63 **"At that point,"** Conrad p. 146.

P. 63 **"Eight days in a garbage can"**; Conrad quote, Spaceflight DVD Volume 2 @ 41:45.

PP. 63-64 **"Back in Mission Control"** Kraft p. 233.

P. 64 **"Back on the carrier, Gordo and Pete"** Hacker p. 262.

P. 64 **"Son, I ordered it"** LBJ quote; Cooper p. 131.

P. 65 **"Ten o'clock"** Author's note: A nickname given to Wally due to his affinity for having a cup of coffee and a cigarette or two before hitting the flight line in the morning.

P. 65 **"Marking time"** French/Burgess p. 50.

P. 65 **"Gordo had a fairly casual"** Stafford p. 64. Author's note: When Cooper was backup for Stafford on Apollo 10, Deke pulled Stafford aside and said, "Damn it Tom, you'd better not get sick on me." Stafford p. 123.

PP. 65-66 **"As to the current state."** Quotes, Kraft p. 234.


# Chapter 4: 76

PP. 67-68 **"The "Agena target vehicle" was actually"**; Almost entirely paraphrased from Shayler pp. 59-61.

PP. 68-69 **LOR discussion**/Houbolt interview; To The Moon DVD @ 10:26 through 16:35.

P. 69 **"It is still possible"** Author's note: Malaysia Air Flight # 370, was lost March 8, 2014.

P. 69 **"Ahead of him"** Author's note: Or her.

P. 71 **Schirra bio/Childhood**; Schirra p. 10.

P. 71 **"Young Wally earned"** Schirra p. 28.

P. 71 **"Five gallon jug"** From the Earth to the Moon DVD Part 3: We Have Cleared the Tower @ 12:26.

PP. 71-72 **Shepard film gotcha.** Moon Shot DVD Part 2 Episode 3 @ 21:51.

P. 72 **"Film for posterity"** Author's note: Of course there was absolutely no way in hell that a stunt like that was going to go unanswered and, as Wally would soon find out, payback is a bitch when you mess with Alan Shepard. Wally, being an Annapolis man and all, fancied himself quite the sailor and he'd bought a sailboat which he'd christened with the cutesy name "Countdown." One day Shepard rounded up comedian Bill Dana and the rest of his posse and took them down to the marina where Countdown was moored. Once there, Al and the gang moved Wally's baby into a nearby storage shed. Then, they took a mast identical to the one on Wally's boat and rammed it down into the mud of Countdown's slip to where only the top couple of feet stuck out of the water. After that, they had a guy at the marina call Wally to tell him that Countdown appeared to be listing in her slip. Al and the guys then retreated to some nearby bushes where they nearly broke their ribs laughing when Wally showed up and collapsed into a moaning heap on the dock. Recounted at Schefter pp. 266-267.

P. 72 **"In Deke's words"** Slayton p. 158.

P. 72 **"Deke's choice to fly"** Stafford p. 1.

P. 72 **"Developed an interest in aviation"** Stafford p. 4.

P. 73 **"The U.S. Naval Academy where he"** Stafford NASA bio, p. 1.

P. 73 **"From there, he would eventually"** Stafford pp. 36-38.

P. 73 **"Raised to six feet"** Author's Note: It had originally been 5'10" at Lovelace during the Mercury clinical trials.

P. 74 **"The Agena was fueled and ready on Pad 14"** Stafford p. 66.

P. 74 **"When, at 10 o'clock a.m."** Hacker p. 268.

P. 74 **"Horribly wrong with the vehicle"** Hacker p. 268; Kraft p. 236; French/Burgess p. 60.

P. 74 **"Schirra later said felt like"** Schirra p. 158.

P. 74 **"Undoubtedly, there would have"** Kraft p. 236.

P. 74 **""A-ha" moments"** Hacker p. 269; Kraft p. 236.

P. 75 **"Of course, there were unprecedented"** Kraft pp. 236-237; Hacker pp. 272-273.

P. 76 **"Because it carried consumables"** Borman p. 122.

P. 76 **"Disassemble the entire Gemini VI launch vehicle."** Schirra p. 159.

P. 76 **"Borman-perhaps recognizing"** Borman p. 126.

P. 77 **"Frank Frederick Borman II"** Borman p. 13.

P. 77 **Childhood, Early interest in aviation, Tucson High nickname;** Borman pp. 13-15, p. 23.

P. 77 **"In spite of the turbulence"** Borman pp. 19-20.

P. 77 **"Expected of me"** Author's note: Emphasis added.

P. 77 **"West Point demanded"** Borman pp. 31-32.

P. 78 **"Selected to fly second seat"** French/Burgess p. 64.

P. 78 **"He proved just how fascinated"** French/Burgess p. 65.

P. 79 **"Was a classmate of Schirra"** French/Burgess p. 66.

P. 79 **"Anomaly in his liver"** French/Burgess p. 65.

P. 79 **"Two weeks with Frank Borman"** Lovell quote, Moon Shot DVD Part 1 Episode 2 @ 1:22:39.

P. 79 **"The best possible position in orbit"** Borman p. 130.

P. 80 **"Spend two weeks in a men's room"** French/Burgess p. 69.

P. 81 **"There was the problem with their suits"** Hacker p. 28; Borman pp. 136-137.

P. 81 **"45 hours into the flight"** Scratching quote, Kraft p. 240.

P. 81 **"Let both men go pressure—suitless"** Borman p. 137.

P. 81 **"Couldn't you just wait five more days"** Lovell quote: When We Left Earth DVD Episode 2 "Friends and Rivals" @ 35:05.

P. 81 **"The good news"** Hacker p. 282; Borman p. 141.

P. 81 **"Early in the morning"** Stafford p. 70.

P. 82 **"The Titan just sat there"** Stafford p. 70; Schirra p. 161.

P. 82 **"BRFC"** Kranz p. 164.

P. 82 **"Wally employed"** Schirra quote; French/Burgess p. 70.

P. 83 **"It was later determined"** French/Burgess p. 71.

P. 83 **"As for Stafford"** Stafford quote; French/Burgess p. 71.

P. 83 **"While they both could have"** French/Burgess p. 71.

P. 84 **"Beat Army"** gotcha. French/Burgess p. 74 quoting Stafford.

P. 85 **Santa Claus/UFO Gotcha.** French/Burgess p. 75.

P. 85 **"Morale inside the ship was not exactly"** Quote; Moon Shot Part I Episode 2 @ 1:23:01.

P. 85 **"On day twelve"** Hacker p. 292.

P. 86 **"Anything less"** Borman p. 146.

P. 86 **"Welcome home, Squarehead"** Borman p. 23.

## Chapter 5: The Original "Houston, We Have a Problem"

PP. 87-88 **"That problem was named Elliot See"** quote; Slayton p. 167.

P. 88 **"Who Deke deemed"** quote; Slayton p. 167.

P. 88 **"Bum decision"/"Let myself get sentimental about Elliott"** Slayton p. 167.

P. 88 **"Flying NASA T-38 aircraft"** Riveting account of See/Bassett crash at Stafford pp. 80-81.

P. 89 **"Neil A. Armstrong"** Armstrong NASA bio, p. 1.

P. 89 **"Recurrent dream"** quote; Hansen p. 46.

P. 89 **"Academically, Neil was such a whiz"** Hansen p. 30.

P. 90 **"Like Frank Borman"** Hansen p. 52.

P. 90 **Armstrong Bio/Teenager/Purdue/Holloway plan** Hansen p. 56, p. 62.

P. 90 **"Flew 78 combat missions"**, Hansen p. 112.

P. 90, **"(NACA) and had landed a test pilot job"** Armstrong NASA bio. p. 1.

P. 90 **"The legendary X-15"** Hansen p. 145.

P. 90, **"There was also no questioning Armstrong's nerve"** Hansen p. 94.

P. 91 **Flying Bedstead episode/Armstrong's description/May 6, 1968**; Hansen p. 329.

P. 91 **Group 3 Astronaut Alan Bean's account of Armstrong's behavior after the LLTV crash.** Hansen p. 332; Bean interview, In the Shadow of the Moon DVD @ 30:14.

P. 91 **Early life/Scott NASA bio.** Scott p. 12.

P. 91 **"Record breaking swimmer"** Scott p. 19.

P. 91 **"Accepting an appointment to the U.S. Military Academy"** Scott p. 26.

P. 92 **"Stationed in Europe until 1960"** Scott pp. 50-51.

P. 92 **"Mortified to find that he had instead been tapped to be a professor"** Scott pp. 63-65.

P. 92 **"ARPS at Edwards,"** Scott pp. 75-76.

PP. 92-93 **"The primary mission objective"/EVA/Discussion of flight plan;** Hacker pp. 297-305.

P. 93 **"ESP" discussed.** French/Burgess p. 79.

P. 93 **"Over 300 zero-G parabolas"** Hacker p. 305.

P. 93 **"While Armstrong was perched atop"** Scott p. 151.

P. 94 **"Forced Chris Kraft to bid" "I'd trained them"** quote; Kraft p. 253.

P. 94 **Agena 8 launch.** Hacker p. 308; Scott p. 163; Hansen p. 246; French/Burgess p. 83.

P. 94 **Launch description by Scott.** Scott p. 163.

P. 94 **"Catch up to the target vehicle"** Hanson p. 247.

PP. 94-95 **"Over the course of the next four or so hours"** French/Burgess p. 83; Hansen p. 250; Hacker p. 310.

PP. 94-95 **Rendezvous and stationkeeping/docking sequence.** Hansen pp. 251-257; French/Burgess pp. 83-85; Scott pp. 165-172; Kranz pp. 171-172; Kraft pp. 253-256.

P. 96 **"Then, as Chris Kraft"** Kraft p. 254.

P. 96 **"After losing comm with Lovell"** Scott p. 166.

P. 96 **"Neil, we're in a bank"** quote; Hacker p. 312.

P. 96 **"Left roll"** Scott p. 167.

P. 96 **"Neil and Dave were spinning counterclockwise"** Hansen pp. 259-260; French/Burgess p. 85; Hacker p. 312; Scott pp. 166-167.

P. 97 **"Silver baton"** quote. Scott p. 6.

P. 97 **"… Undock NOW!"** Scott p. 167.

PP. 97-98 **"As Gene Kranz pointed out"** quote; Kranz p. 172.

P. 98 **"Firing Gemini thrusters."** Author's note: It was actually only one thruster—#8—causing the problem.

P. 98 **Reacquisition of signal by CSQ CapCom.** Hansen p. 261; Hacker p. 314; Scott p. 167; French/Burgess p. 85.

P. 98 **"All we've got left"** Armstrong quote; Hacker p. 315.

P. 98 **"Mission rules dictated"** French/Burgess p. 87.

P. 99 **"Hodge didn't blink"** Hacker p. 315.

P. 99 **"South China Sea with recovery to be made"** Hansen p. 263.

P. 99 **"Out in the wilderness"** quote; French/Burgess p. 8; Hansen p. 263.

P. 99 **"Having seen Hodge have his ass"** Hacker p. 317.

P. 100 **"Armstrong and Scott had to endure"** Scott pp. 174-178.

P. 100 **"In the aftermath"** French/Burgess p. 88; Hacker p. 319; Kranz p. 174.

P. 100 **"Oams Thruster # 8"** Hacker p. 321.


# Chapter 6: These Boots Ain't Made for Walkin'

P. 104 **"Been declared a non-entity"** Scott p. 99.

PP. 104-105 **"Sergei Pavlovich Korolev"** Scott pp. 138-144; Death of—Burrows pp. 402-404.

P. 104 **"Recognizing his immense value"** Scott p. 53.

P. 105 **Hail Mary pass/Puncher's chance.** Author's note: Sorry about the sports metaphors but this is a race we're talking about, right?

P. 107 **"White Team (Kranz's) flight controller"** Author's note: Mission Control's White Team was led by Gene Kranz.

P. 107 **"If it was up to me"** Llewellyn quote, Race to the Moon Vol. 1/History Channel Failure Is Not an Option DVD @ 32:19.

P. 108 **Llewellyn characteristics** Kranz p. 121; **Judo** Kranz p. 129.

P. 108 **Llewellyn/Shepard, riding horse to work incidents**; Kranz p. 129 (Shepard) Kranz p. 162 (Horse riding).

PP. 108-109 **"The Air Force had developed"/AMU discussion.** Hacker p. 325.

P. 109 **"Daniel McKee"** Hacker p. 326.

P. 110 **"As to Gemini IX's other mission objectives"** Hacker p. 329.

P. 110 **"During the third orbit"** Hacker p. 327.

P. 110 **"Eugene Andrew "Gene" Cernan."** French/Burgess p. 92.

P. 110 **"That, by definition, meant naval aviation"** French/Burgess p. 92.

P. 110 **"Chased his dream to Purdue University"** Cernan pp. 24-26.

P. 111 **"A real naval aviator"** Cernan p. 49.

P. 111 **"Two years later"** French/Burgess p. 91.

P. 111 **"With no input whatsoever from him"** Cernan p. 52.

P. 111 **"Imposter Astronaut"** French/Burgess pp. 92-93.

P. 111 **"An honor"** French/Burgess p. 93.

P. 112 **Agena launch failure/Gemini IX launch abort.** French/Burgess p. 95; Kraft p. 258.

P. 112 **"It isn't 'Aw shucks'"** Kraft p. 258.

P. 112 **"That night, an Air Force lieutenant colonel"** Stafford p. 86.

P. 112 **"Ever since the Agena failure"** Hacker p. 331.

P. 112 **"A hybrid contraption called"; ATDA described.** French/Burgess p. 95.

P. 112 **ATDA launch/telemetry signals; Shroud problem** French/Burgess p. 96; Hacker p. 332.

P. 113 **"The Titan abruptly refused to accept"** French/Burgess p. 96; Hacker p. 332.

P. 113 **"Mayor of Pad 19"** Cernan p. 115.

P. 113 **"On June 3, 1966"** French/Burgess p. 96; Hacker p. 332.

P. 113 **" NASA humor"** Cernan p. 115.

P. 113 **"Some smartass"** Cernan p. 116.

P. 113 **"We were kidding before"** Cernan p. 116.

P. 114 **"Cold day in hell"** Cernan p. 116.

P. 114 **"Gemini IX roared to life"** Hacker p. 332; Kranz p. 181; Cernan p. 117; French/Burgess p. 96.

P. 114 **"Kranz's first thought"** quote; Kranz p. 181.

P. 114 **"Stafford had the ground back off "** Hacker p. 334.

P. 115 **"Had been taped down"** Stafford p. 90.

P. 115 **"Give it a nudge"** Kranz p. 182.

P. 115 **"Went home for supper"** Kranz p. 182.

P. 115 **"Why the hell Lunney wasn't in Lunney's chair"** Kranz p. 182.

P. 115 **"What EVA?"** Kranz p. 182.

P. 115 **"Taking the steps two at a time"** Kranz p. 183.

P. 116 **"So livid"/"Get himself under control"** Kranz p. 183.

P. 116 **"Buzz had pitched the idea"/"Snip the tape"** Cernan p. 123.

P. 116 **"Kranz gave an impassioned response"** Kranz p. 183.

P. 116 **"No way"** Stafford p. 91.

P. 117 **"Pretty well bushed"** Cernan p. 126; Stafford p. 91.

PP. 118-120 **Cernan EVA/Spacewalk from hell**. Kranz p. 186; Cernan pp. 130-143; French/Burgess pp. 98-101; Kraft pp. 259-260; Stafford pp. 91-93; Hacker pp. 337-339.

P. 118 **"A lesson in Newton's Laws"** quote; Cernan pp. 132-133.

P. 119 **"Like a balloon in the Macy's parade"** quote/Suit inflexibility, Cernan p. 134; Hacker p. 338; Stafford p. 91; French/Burgess p. 99.

P. 119 **"Now his vision was compromised?"** Hacker pp. 338-339; French/Burgess pp. 99-101; Cernan p. 137; Stafford pp. 92-93.

P. 120 **"Putting a champagne cork back in a champagne bottle"** French/Burgess p. 101.

P. 120 **"Like a guy doing the limbo"** Cernan p. 142.

P. 120 **"Helmet to helmet"** Stafford p. 93; Hacker p. 339.

P. 120 **Stafford pre-flight conversation with Slayton about not cutting Cernan loose if he died outside the spacecraft on EVA.** Stafford p. 88.

P. 121 **"Geno, how could you give a shit?"** Stafford p. 96.

P. 121 **"No atheists in foxholes or spacecrafts going through reentry"** Cernan p. 148.

P. 121 **"Post flight debriefing"** Cernan p. 152.

P. 121 **"Ticker-tape adulation"** Cernan p. 155.

## Chapter 7: Enter the Renaissance Man

P. 123 **"Slept like a baby"** Collins p. 198.

P. 123 **"Michael "Mike" Collins"** French/Burgess pp. 104-105.

P. 124 **"Lemming-like"** French/Burgess p. 105.

P. 124 **Mailer quote,** French/Burgess p. 105.

P. 125 **"They must be out of their minds."** Hacker p. 42.

PP. 125-126 **Discussion of Gemini X mission objectives.** Young p. 88.

P. 125 **"After getting Mike"** Author's Note: Gemini VIII's Agena hereinafter referred to as "Agena 8"; Gemini X's Agena will henceforth be referred to as "Agena 10"; Also, Collins initial stand-up EVA would not be performed until after the rendezvous with Agena 10 during the actual mission.

P. 126 **"Urine collection bag"/Pre-flight ritual.** Collins p. 198.

P. 126 **"Bring a pair of pliers along"** French/Burgess p. 104.

P. 127 **"Sigh of relief"** Collins p. 202.

P. 127 **"As Kraft, Hodge and Kranz"** Hacker p. 334.

P. 127 **Gemini X launch.** Young p. 89; Collins p. 203; Hacker p. 344; French/Burgess p. 106.

P. 127 **"Lunney had the Capcom radio up"** Hacker p. 344.

P. 127 **"Trying to keep his buddy's head up"** Collins p. 208.

P. 127 **Rendezvous sequence with Agena 10.** French/Burgess p. 107; Young p. 91; Hacker p. 344.

P. 128, **"Whifferdil"** Young p. 91.

P. 128 **"Goddammit, we know that"** Collins p. 210.

P. 128 **"Added redundancy in the propulsion department"** Author's note: That redundancy would pay the ultimate dividend on Apollo 13.

P. 128, **"Eyeballs out"** Young p. 93; Collins p. 211; Hacker p. 345.

P. 128 **"It's pretty damn hard to talk"** Young p. 93.

P. 128 **"For 80 seconds"** Author's note: French/Burgess and Hacker both say 80 seconds. Collins says 14 seconds. The Gemini X air to ground transcript is unclear.

P. 129 **Window shades/Trouble sleeping/Hands in mouth.** Collins p. 216.

P. 129 **"Beginning their pursuit of Agena 8"** Collins p. 217; Young p. 92.

P. 129 **Slayton/Crew exchange.** Collins p. 219.

P. 130 **"Jesus Christ! Here I am"** Collins p. 219.

P. 130 **"The Stand-up EVA".** Author's note: Young's memoir p. 96 notes that both hatches were open during the stand-up EVA. Neither Collins, French/Burgess or Hacker confirm John's account.

P. 130 **Stand up EVA/Eye-burning problem** Collins p. 222; Young p. 94; French/Burgess p. 108.

P. 130 **"Pegged the problem as both"** Hacker p. 348.

PP. 130-133 **A10 Undocking/A8 rendezvous and docking/ Collins EVA.** French/Burgess pp. 109-111; Hacker pp. 348-350; Collins pp. 226-238; Young pp. 95-100.

P. 133 **"Come back in the house"** Young p. 99.

P. 133 **"Super retro"** Collins p. 246.

P. 133 **"All four retros had fired"** Young p. 101; French/Burgess p. 111; Hacker p. 350.

PP. 133-134 **Post flight bunny story;** Collins p. 252.

## Chapter 8: 850 Down; 239,150 To Go

P. 137 **"Richard F. "Dick" Gordon"** Gordon NASA bio; French/Burgess pp. 113-114.

P. 138 **"Sympathizing with his friend's frustration"** French/Burgess p. 114; Conrad p. 148.

P. 138 **"The Animal"** Author's note: For the record, Gordon was never particularly fond of the whole "The Animal" thing. Because it was Conrad that came up with it, Dick tolerated it. It's unlikely the nickname would've flown had it come from anyone other than Pete.

P. 139 **"Virtually inseparable" quoting Guenter Wendt.** French/Burgess p. 114.

PP. 139-141 **Mission objectives/M=1/EVA/Hearing Russian footsteps.** Hacker pp. 354-356.

P. 139 **"Emergency free lunar voyage"** Author's note: i.e. A "routine" mission—as if any flight from the Earth to the moon could be characterized in such a way.

P. 139 **"Prior to coming home"** Author's note: The return to Earth would be initiated by executing a maneuver called "transearth injection."

P. 140 **Nixed lunar flyaround/Conrad getting NASA to sign off on going up to set the altitude record.** Hacker pp. 354-355.

P. 140 **Tether flight experiment.** Hacker pp. 355-356.

P. 141 **"September 12, 1966"/Launch.** Hacker p. 358; French/ Burgess p. 116.

P. 141 **"Dick radioed, "Tell Mr. Kraft"** Kraft p. 262.

P. 141 **Docking/Redocking maneuvers.** Hacker p. 359; French/ Burgess p. 116.

P. 141 **"Unable to undertake"** Author's note: Because of X's excessive fuel consumption during their initial rendezvous maneuvers.

P. 142 **"Have thrown Pete"** Gordon quote, French/Burgess p. 116.

P. 142 **"Day two, as Chris Kraft"** Kraft p. 262.

P. 142 **"Fully suited and awaiting the start."** Hacker p. 360; French/Burgess pp. 116-117.

P. 142 **"Hatch opening"/"Dick was already gassed".** Hacker p. 361; French/Burgess p. 118.

P. 143 **Shutting down Gordon's EVA.** Slayton p. 179; Kraft p. 262; French/Burgess p. 118; Hacker pp. 361-362.

P. 143 **Conrad's fear of having to cut Gordon loose and come home alone.** Conrad p. 150.

P. 143 **"After successfully completing the climb."** Slayton p. 180; Kraft p. 263; French/Burgess p. 119; Hacker p. 363.

P. 144 **Stand-up EVA/Falling asleep.** French/Burgess p. 120; Hacker p. 366.

P. 144 **"Mere feet of each other."** Author's note: This had to be the most harebrained stunt in Gemini, if not NASA, history and considering the daredevilish nature of some of Gemini's EVAs that's saying something.

P. 144 **Conduct of "great tether experiment."** French/Burgess p. 121; Hacker pp. 366-367.

P. 145 **Last Agena rendezvous.** Hacker p. 369.

## Chapter 9: Bringing Down the Curtain

P. 147 **"Command assignments for Gemini's IX through XI"** Slayton p. 168.

P. 148 **"In a way, it was the shittiest"** Aldrin pp. 152-153.

PP. 148-149, **"Buzz was born."** Aldrin NASA bio, French/ Burgess p. 123.

P. 148 **"Shortened that to Buzz."** Author's note: Later in life, Buzz would change his legal name to "Buzz Aldrin."

P. 149 **"Buzz then cut his aviation teeth"** French/Burgess p. 124, Aldrin NASA Bio.

P. 149 **Schirra story of Aldrin Group 3 interview.** Moon Shot DVD, Part 1 Episode 2 @ 1:30:51.

P. 150 **"Lack of 'intellectual curiosity'"** French/Burgess p. 125.

P. 150 **"No one wanted to be seated next to"** Alan Bean Interview/In the Shadow of the Moon DVD @ 29:12. Author's note: The astronaut couple who invited Buzz over for the ill-fated evening were Walter Cunningham and his wife Lo. Chaikin p. 143.

P. 150 **"By mid-1965"** Aldrin p. 114.

P. 151 **"Had the self-awareness to admit"** Aldrin pp. 144-145.

P. 151 **"In order to make that happen"** Slayton p. 180.

P. 151 **"First came modifications to the training procedures"** Hacker pp. 370-373.

P. 152 **"Underwater neutral buoyancy training"** Kraft p. 263; Hacker pp. 370-373.

P. 152 **"Threw a Gemini capsule into a swimming pool"** Moon Shot DVD Part 1 Episode 2 @ 1:31:24.

P. 152 **"Not mine"** Aldrin quote, French/Burgess p. 128.

P. 153 **"Only part of the new EVA equation"** Hacker pp. 320-323.

P. 153 **"The" "End"** Aldrin p. 169; Slayton p. 181.

P. 154 **"Using only a sextant"** French/Burgess p. 131; Hacker p. 375.

P. 154 **"Mark one cranium computer"** Aldrin p. 172.

P. 154 **"Anomaly with the turbine pump"** Hacker p. 376; French/Burgess p. 131.

P. 155 **EVA 1.** Hacker p. 377; Aldrin p. 173; French/Burgess p. 181.

PP. 155-156 **EVA 2.** Hacker p. 378; Aldrin p. 176; French/Burgess p. 132.

P. 156 **"Would you change the oil, too?"** Author's note: Ah, a full-service filling station reference. How quaint.

P. 156 **EVA 3.** French/Burgess p. 133; Hacker p. 378.

P. 156 **Ali message.** Author's note: And Ali still is "The Greatest."

P. 157 **"Gemini developed the tools"** Kranz p. 190.

PP. 157-158 **"As for the race to the moon"** Kraft p. 265. Author's note: Author David Whitehouse states, "…the United Press International Agency reported that the Soviet Union would launch a multi-crewed spacecraft before the end of March 1966, in time for the 23rd Congress of the Communist Party. This was the planned Voskhod 3 mission, by which they intended to regain the duration record. It was to be an outstanding publicity victory for the Soviet's space program, but long-duration ground tests of the life-support system did not go well. After fourteen days, the Institute for Biomedical Problems had to abandon them because of a worsening of the cabin atmosphere. Parachute failures during recovery tests were common. Four cosmonauts were in training for the flight but as the problems accumulated it became increasingly clear that there might never be a Voskhod 3 mission. Soon it was cancelled." Whitehouse @ p. 151.

P. 158 **"My view is simple"** Kraft p. 265.


# Epilogue

P. 159 **"There had been difficulties"** Leopold pp. 226-227.

P. 159 **"Lemon"** Leopold p. 234.

P. 159 **"If you have a glitch or any kind of anomaly"** Schirra interview Moon Shot DVD Part II Episode 3 "Go Fever" @ 12:46.

P. 160 **Comm problems.** Leopold p. 249.

P. 160 **6:31 pm.** Leopold pp. 249-251.

P. 160 **Apollo 1 fire described.** Chaikin pp. 12-18.

P. 161 **"Marking time"** Slayton p. 168.

P. 163 **"LM was not yet ready"** Author's note: Obviously, a landing could not be attempted.

P. 166 **"Son of a bitch"** Cernan p. 217.

P. 166 **Cernan helicopter crash.** Cernan p. 258.

P. 167 **"I wish that son of a bitch"** Author's note: In Tom Hanks' "From the Earth to the Moon," the Gordon character spoke those words. Gordon's actual words at hatch closing were "I guess I've gotta close the hatch now." Chaikin p. 256.

P. 168 **"Rubbed the wrong way"** Author's note: Or flat-out pissed off.

PP. 169-170 **"Post-Apollo 14 brandy with his father"** Shepard interview Moon Shot DVD Part 2 Episode 4 "And never give up" @ 1:21:54.

P. 170 **"Held hundreds in his audience spellbound"** Author's note: Including your author.

P. 170 **"In the U.S. space program"** Author's note: And a hell of a lot of other things.

# About the Author

Bart Colomb was born and raised in Louisville, Kentucky and currently resides in Southern Indiana with his wife, Kelly. He obtained a B.A. in Government and History from Centre College of Kentucky and a J.D. from The Brandeis School of Law at The University of Louisville. Bart retired in 2017 after practicing law for 30 years as a trial attorney. He is a long time member of the National Space Society and the Smithsonian Air and Space Society. *When The Race Was Won* is his first book.

Printed in Dunstable, United Kingdom